18.	Sir Richard Cooke	—	Anne Peyton
19.	William Cooke, Esq.	—	Lettice Fisher
20.	Arthur Cooke, Esq.	—	Margaret Sacheverell
21.	Walsingham Cooke, Esq.	—	Anne Bower
22.	Frederick? Proctor	—	Frances Cooke
23.	William Moore	—	Frances Proctor
24.	Walsingham Moore, Gentleman	—	Frances Proctor (cousin)
25.	Mark Moore	—	Anne Elliott
26.	Walsingham Proctor Moore	—	Fanny Gillon
27.	Ralph Henry Moore, Sr.	—	Blanche Eloise Rosenwater
28.	Ralph Henry Moore, Jr.	—	Estelle Marguerite Hero
29.	Thomas Ronald Moore, Esq.	—	Margaret Clarissa King
30.	Willard Sean Moore, Esq.	—	Margaret Else Nelson, Esq.

Elizabeth Margaret Clarissa Moore

Charles Ralph Henry Moore

31. Sarah Elizabeth Moore

PLANTAGENET DESCENT

PLANTAGENET DESCENT

31 Generations
from
William the Conqueror
to
Today

THOMAS R. MOORE

GATEWAY PRESS, INC.
Baltimore, MD   1995

Copyright © 1995 by Thomas R. Moore
All rights reserved.

Permission to reproduce in any form
must be secured in writing from the author.

Please direct all correspondence and book orders to:
Plantagenet Descent
1170 Fifth Avenue, Suite 2A
New York, NY 10029

Library of Congress Catalog Card Number 95-75164
ISBN 0-9644929-0-3

∞

This paper meets the requirements of
ANSI/NISO Z39.48-1992
(Permanence of Paper)

Thomas R. Moore, Esq., B.A. magna cum laude,
Yale University, J.D., Harvard University
Subjects: Biography, Genealogy and History:
Charlemagne, William the Conqueror, Plantagenet,
Bohun, Courtenay, Cobham, de la Pole, Braybroke,
Brooke, Peyton, Cooke, Wellesley, Proctor, Moore,
Mayflower, King

Published by:
Gateway Press, Inc.
1001 N. Calvert Street
Baltimore, MD 21202

Printed in the United States of America

To
The Future

Contents

Illustrations begin many of the chapters

Dramatis Personae xv
Chapter 1: William the Conqueror and Matilda 1
Chapter 2: King Henry I and Princess Matilda 13
Chapter 3: Geoffrey Plantagenet* Count of Anjou and
              Matilda the Empress 17
Chapter 4: King Henry II and Eleanor of Aquitaine 21
Chapter 5: King John and Isabella 25
Chapter 6: King Henry III and Eleanor 29
Chapter 7: King Edward I and Princess Eleanor 37
Chapter 8: Humphrey de Bohun VIII, Earl of Hereford and
              Essex, and Her Royal Highness Princess Elizabeth Plantagenet 41
Chapter 9: Hugh de Courtenay Earl of Devon and Lady
              Margaret de Bohun 45
Chapter 10: John de Cobham 3d Baron Cobham and Lady
              Margaret de Courtenay 51
Chapter 11: Sir John de la Pole and Lady Joane de Cobham 59
Chapter 12: Sir Reginald de Braybroke Knight Banneret and
              Lady Joane de la Pole 4th Baron(ess) Cobham . . 67
Chapter 13: Sir Thomas Brooke and Lady Joane de Braybroke 5th Baron(ess) Cobham 73
Chapter 14: Reginald Brooke, Esq., younger brother of Sir
              Edward Brooke 6th Baron Cobham, and Anne
              Evelyn 81

---

* Geoffrey Plantagenet was so called because of his habit of wearing in his helmet a sprig of the golden broom plant (planta: sprig, genêt: broom plant). The name "Plantagenet" is used by historians as a surname for the line of English kings Geoffrey engendered.

Contents

Chapter 15: Francis Peyton, Esq., and Elizabeth Brooke .. 85
Chapter 16: Christopher Peyton, Esq., and Joanne Mildmay 91
Chapter 17: Christopher Peyton, Esq., Auditor General in Ireland, and Alice Newman 101
Chapter 18: Sir Richard Cooke, Principal Secretary of State and Chancellor of the Exchequer in Ireland, and Anne Peyton 105
Chapter 19: William Cooke, Esq., First Master of the Dublin Goldsmiths' Company, and Lettice Fisher . . . 115
Chapter 20: Arthur Cooke, Esq., and Margaret Sacheverell . 125
Chapter 21: Walsingham Cooke, Esq., and Anne Bower . . 127
Chapter 22: Frederick? Proctor and Frances Cooke 131
Chapter 23: William Moore and Frances Proctor 133
Chapter 24: Walsingham Moore, gentleman, and his first cousin Frances Proctor 145
Chapter 25: Mark Moore and Anne Elliott in Canada . . . 157
Chapter 26: W(alsingham) Proctor Moore and Fanny Gillon 163
Chapter 27: Ralph Henry Moore, Sr. and Blanche Eloise Rosenwater in the United States 167
Chapter 28: Ralph Henry (Jack) Moore, Jr. and Estelle Marguerite Hero 175
Chapter 29: Thomas R(onald) Moore, Esq., and Margaret Clarissa King 187
Chapter 30: Willard Sean Moore, Esq., and Margaret Else Nelson, Esq., Elizabeth Margaret Clarissa Moore, Charles Ralph Henry Moore 197
Chapter 31: Sarah Elizabeth Moore 199
Appendix 201
Notes 205
Selected Bibliography 221
Key Sources 223
Index 225

Illustrations

Family Tree	Endsheet
Map	Endsheet
William the Conqueror	Ch. 1
The Tower of London, Palace of William the Conqueror	Ch. 1
King Henry I mourning the death of his only legitimate son in the wreck of the White Ship	Ch. 2
Count Geoffrey Plantagenet who at 14 married the Empress Matilda, daughter and heir of King Henry I	Ch. 2
Eleanor of Aquitaine (wife of King Henry II) and her daughter-in-law Isabella of Angoulême (13 year old bride of King John and mother of King Henry III)	Ch. 2
King Henry III	Ch. 2
King Henry II (first Plantagenet King and great-grandson of William the Conqueror) disputing with Becket	Ch. 4
King John	Ch. 5
King Edward I	Ch. 7
The Palace of King Edward I	Ch. 7
The Throne of King Edward I	Ch. 7
Coat of arms of Humphrey de Bohun, Earl of Hereford and Essex, husband of Her Royal Highness Princess Elizabeth Plantagent	Ch. 7
Coat of arms of Hugh de Courtenay, Earl of Devon, husband of Lady Margaret de Bohun	Ch. 7
Lord Cobham, John de Cobham, 3d Baron Cobham	Ch. 10
Lady Margaret de Courtenay (daughter of the Earl of Devon), Lord Cobham's wife	Ch. 10
Cooling (Cowling) Castle, seat of the Lords Cobham	Ch. 10

Illustrations

Sir John de la Pole and Lady Joane de Cobham	Ch. 11
Sir Reginald de Braybroke, Knight Banneret	Ch. 12
Lady Joane de la Pole, Baroness Cobham, his wife	Ch. 12
Wills of Sir Thomas Broke and of his son Sir Thomas Brooke "lord of Cobham"	Ch. 13
Margaret Francis, mother of Francis Peyton, Esq.	Ch. 15
Moulsham Hall	Ch. 16
Sir Thomas Mildmay	Ch. 16
Sir Walter Mildmay	Ch. 16
Sir Francis Walsingham (uncle of Christopher Peyton, Auditor General, and of Sir Richard Cooke) with Queen Elizabeth I	Ch. 16
Arms of Christopher Peyton, Esq., Auditor General in Ireland	Ch. 17
Arms of Sir Richard Cooke, Knight, Principal Secretary of State and Chancellor of the Exchequer	Ch. 17
Silver Chalice in St. Werburgh's Church, Dublin, in 1993, created by William Cooke, Esq. in 1641	Ch. 17
Arms of Margaret Sacheverell, wife of Arthur Cooke	Ch. 17
Arthur Wellesley, Duke of Wellington	Ch. 24
Mark Moore and Anne Elliott, c. 1865	Ch. 25
Walsingham Proctor Moore, Fanny Gillon, and 3 month old son Mark Alfred Moore, Carleton Place, Ontario, 5 June 1872	Ch. 26
Ralph Henry Moore, Sr. in Duluth, Minn. c. 1893, and Blanche Eloise Rosenwater in Kennett, Mo. c. 1898	Ch. 27
Ralph Henry Moore, Jr. and Estelle Marguerite Hero, 1930	Ch. 28
Thomas R. Moore	Ch. 29
Margaret Clarissa King	Ch. 29
Arms of Thomas R. Moore	Ch. 29
Willard Sean Moore	Ch. 29

Illustrations

Margaret Else Nelson . . . . Ch. 29
Elizabeth Margaret Clarissa Moore . . . . Ch. 29
Charles Ralph Henry Moore . . . . Ch. 29
Sarah Elizabeth Moore . . . . Ch. 29
Arms of Margaret Clarissa King . . . . Ch. 29

Preface

Shortly before the death of Napoleon's nemesis the Duke of Wellington, Sir William Betham—Ulster King of Arms—compiled the Registered Pedigree of William Cooke and his son Sir Richard Cooke and wife Anne Peyton. This Registered Pedigree, currently recorded in the Genealogical Office in Dublin, traces her ancestry back to Princess Elizabeth Plantagenet, daughter of King Edward I of England, and forward to the Duke of Wellington, to his brother the Marquess Wellesley who became the ancestor of Queen Elizabeth II of England, and to Frances Cooke who became the ancestress of the author.

Mr. Moore's book fleshes out and brings to life the 31 generations from William the Conqueror and his Queen Matilda (both descendants of the Emperor Charlemagne), through the royalty, nobility and gentry of England, through the Elizabethan Age, through high offices in Ireland to William Moore who came to Canada in 1817, then down one line of his estimated 55,000 descendants alive today* to the contemporary joyous productive professional and personal lives of the author and his family, including a baby granddaughter, in Manhattan.

Many share part of the same history and genealogy but lack the records to know it. All, however, can revel in this true story.

---

* Assuming that 5 children were born to each of his 6 children, 5 children to each of their descendants for the next 2 generations, 3 children to each for the next 3 generations, and 2 children to each for the current generation, that 90 percent of these births had only one parent descended from William Moore (i.e. 10 percent cousin marriages) and that 90 percent of the last 3 generations are still alive and none of the preceding generations.

Dramatis Personae

Other than the Kings and Queens of England (Chapters 1–7), two of the seminal historical figures in this book are Sir Francis Walsingham (Chapter 16) and Anne Peyton (Chapter 18). And the most exciting person is Joane de la Pole (Chapter 12), born into England's richest merchant family, orphaned and married at age one, a mother and widow at 12, a baroness at 29, married to the most controversial figure of the century within the year; she married five times, and had 11 children, one of whom survived her to become the 5th Baron(ess) Cobham (Chapter 13).

Anne Peyton's family had lived in Suffolk, England, in Isleham or nearby Bury St. Edmunds, for at least nine generations before her father, Christopher Peyton, Esq., went to Ireland under Queen Elizabeth I to serve as Auditor General. Her great-great-grandparents, Thomas Peyton and Margaret Francis, are depicted in 3-foot brasses in Isleham Church (near Cambridge), he in armor and she in long dress and butterfly head-dress, from which gorgeous rubbings, of which I have one, were still being made in the late 20th century. An illustration of Margaret begins Chapter 15.

Anne Peyton married Sir Richard Cooke and became the ancestress of the Cooke-Proctor-Moore line, of which I am a descendant. After Sir Richard died, Anne married Sir Henry Colley and engendered the Colley-Wellesley line that includes Arthur Wellesley the great Duke of Wellington and Queen Elizabeth II. I have had the pleasure of serving on a corporate board of directors with the 8th Duke of Wellington, Arthur Valerian Wellesley, and visiting him at the ducal seat of Stratfield Saye. Anne Peyton's sister-in-law Mary Colley married Sir Garret Moore, Viscount Moore of Drogheda, whose grandson became the 1st Earl of

Dramatis Personae

Drogheda. Derry Moore, the noted photographer, is the current and 12th Earl of Drogheda.

Sir Francis Walsingham was one of the giant statesmen of Elizabethan England, an architect of her foreign policy who became Principal Secretary of State in 1573. From a genealogical point of view, he inspired his nephew, the above-mentioned Sir Richard Cooke, who left England to serve as Chancellor of the Exchequer and Lord Chief Baron and Principal Secretary of State in Ireland following his uncle's death, to name his firstborn, by Anne Peyton, "Walsingham." Sir Walsingham Cooke held the office of High Sheriff (duties similar to those of an earl in earlier times) in Tomduff, co. Wexford. The name "Walsingham" has since regularly recurred in the Cooke-Proctor-Moore line in the succeeding four centuries.[1]

Of the 31 generations discussed in this book, Sir Richard Cooke (Chapter 18) is one of the persons to whom I would most like to talk. As noted, he married Anne Peyton, a direct descendant of the English Kings William the Conqueror through Edward I, and a direct ancestress of the Duke of Wellington, Queen Elizabeth II, and myself. In his own right, besides becoming Chancellor of the Exchequer and Lord Chief Baron and Principal Secretary of State and a knight, he amassed over 7,300 acres of land, more than 11 square miles, nearly triple the holdings of the Lords Cobham (Chapters 10–13). Their great-great-great-granddaughter (the daughter of Frances Cooke) married William Moore (Chapter 23) about 1766, to whom I would most like to talk.

This book covers a thousand years of dramatic events.

William the Conqueror

The Tower of London
Palace of William the Conqueror

Chapter 1

William the Conqueror (1027–1087)
m. 1053
Matilda of Flanders (c. 1032–1083)

He was called William the Bastard before he became William the Conqueror. He was born in Falaise in what is now northern France on 14 October 1027, the illegitimate son of Robert the Devil, Duke of Normandy, and Arlette, daughter of a tanner of Falaise. His parents lived together from the moment Robert discovered Arlette washing in the river.

Robert was the established ruler of one of the groups of Northmen (Norsemen, Normans) who had come from Norway and Denmark to conquer and settle eastern England and northern France over the preceding several centuries*. The Normans achieved stability in France in 911 when the King of France concluded a treaty with Rollo, duke of the Normans. Rollo was baptized in 912. Robert the Devil was his great-great-grandson.

When Robert the Devil went on a pilgrimage to Jerusalem about 1035, he had his barons swear fealty to his infant son. Robert died in July 1035 in Nicaea, while returning from that pilgrimage, and William the Bastard became Duke of Normandy at the age of seven. Many of his barons despised him for his low birth and his youth. They killed his three guardians and his tutor

---

* "From the fury of the Norsemen, Good Lord deliver us," was to become a heart-felt litany.

and tried to seize him, but his mother's brother spirited him away and concealed him in the dwellings of the poor. On the advice of loyal lords, he appointed Ralph de Wacy, one of the murderers, as his guardian and as the commander of his forces. This bought him time. Finally, in 1047, at the age of 20, he aligned himself with his sovereign, King Henry I of France (whose niece he would soon marry), and together they crushed the disloyal rebels, securing William's power throughout Normandy.

In 1002 William the Bastard's great-grandfather, the then Duke of Normandy, had caused his daughter Emma to be married to King Ethelred the Unready of England[*]. This was the second marriage for Ethelred who had several children, including Edmund Ironside, by his first marriage. King Ethelred and Queen Emma had two sons, the elder of whom was Edward, later to be known as the Confessor because of his piety. When the Danes overran all of England in 1013, Queen Emma and her infant sons fled to the court of the Duke of Normandy. When Queen Emma returned to England the next year, her two sons remained at the Norman court, to be educated, where they stayed until 1042. Thus Edward lived at the Norman court from about age 10 to age 39. On 23 April 1016 King Ethelred died in London while fighting Canute, the Danish invader. The struggle was continued by his son by his first marriage, King Edmund Ironside, who was killed in the same year. Thereupon Queen Emma married Canute on 2 July 1017 with the stipulation that their son, if one was born to them, would succeed Canute as King of England, to the exclusion of the issue of King Ethelred the Unready. Two decades later, King Canute died in 1035. Edward the Confessor sent his younger brother Alfred to England in 1036 to probe Edward's acceptability

---

[*] Weir, pp. 3–4, gives his ascent back to King Egbert first King of England (c. 769–4 February 839) who is buried in Winchester Cathedral. Egbert's wife Redburga was the sister of Charlemagne.

as king. Canute's son, King Harold, had Godwine, Earl of Wessex, capture Alfred, who was intentionally blinded and soon died of his wounds. Edward, though he would marry Godwine's daughter nine years later, and would bequeath the kingship to Godwine's son 30 years later, never forgave Godwine for Alfred's death. King Canute's sons, King Harold and King Harthacnut, died in 1040 and 1042. In 1042 Edward returned to England to claim the crown. His cousin, the 15 year old William the Bastard, Duke of Normandy, was one of his stoutest supporters. Soon after becoming king, Edward the Confessor seized his mother's fortune "because she had done less for him than he would, both before he became king and also since," in the words of the Anglo-Saxon Chronicle. Edward let her live quietly, in Winchester, where she is buried with Canute in the Cathedral.

King Edward the Confessor was, as noted, a pious man. In 1045, he married the young and beautiful Edith, daughter of Godwine, Earl of Wessex, the most powerful man in England. Despite Edith's youth and beauty, Edward announced, to the delight of the monkish chroniclers, that he had no intention of abandoning his self-imposed celibacy. Thereafter, two men, William the Bastard, Duke of Normandy, and Harold, who succeeded his father as Earl of Wessex in 1053, waited for Edward to die without issue. Death came in 1066.

On his death bed, King Edward the Confessor named Harold, Earl of Wessex and brother of Queen Edith, as his successor. The English witan (council) ratified the choice and Harold was anointed and crowned at Westminster Abbey, which Edward had completed and consecrated the year before. No matter that Edward had been sheltered in the Duke of Normandy's court for nearly 30 years, that he had received the unstinting support of his cousin, William the Bastard, Duke of Normandy, and that he had in 1051 promised the crown to William. No matter that William had forced Harold (when the latter was shipwrecked in France and a virtual prisoner of William) to pledge (over concealed relics) the crown to William. No matter that the English wanted the native-born Harold, not the Norman William, as their king. The succession would be determined by force of arms.

William began to assemble an invasion army of 12,000 men, secured the Pope's blessing (as usual the papacy was incensed with appointments within the English church), and apparently asked the Norwegians to make a simultaneous attack on King Harold.

The English rallied to King Harold, reveling in a native-born king, repelled the Norwegians, made a forced march to meet the Normans near Hastings, and learned that cavalry could defeat infantry. At one point in the battle a rumor spread that William was dead. He ripped off his helmet, showed his face and rallied his troops. As William approached the English line on horseback for the second time, Gyrth, brother of King Harold, threw a spear at him, which hit his charger and killed it. William advanced on foot and killed Gyrth with his own hand. William's mounted troops prevailed, and at the end of the day Harold was dead and England was conquered for the last time.

William had married Matilda, daughter of the Count of Flanders, and niece of the King of France, in 1053. They had three surviving sons: Robert, named for his father's father, and nicknamed "Curthose" (Short Boots) because he was short and fat; William, nicknamed "Rufus" (the red) for his florid complexion; and Henry; and six daughters: one of whom was Adele who married Stephen, Count of Blois, in 1080. Her son Stephen would contest her brother Henry's daughter for the kingship of England, as we shall see in Chapter 3.

On his death bed, the Conqueror, following primogeniture, left Normandy (which he had inherited) to his eldest son Robert Curthose, even though this son had personally led armed rebellions against the father, in one of which he physically wounded his father. The Conqueror left England to his second son William Rufus (the Conqueror's brutal favorite). Son Henry was at his side at his death and in answer to the question, "What lands do you leave to me, Sire?," replied that he had no lands left for him, but that his time would come.

Queen Matilda died in Normandy on 3 November 1083 and was buried in her church at Caen. William the Conqueror died four years later, on 9 September 1087, aged 60, in Rouen, where he had his palace, from a wound he received when his horse stepped on a hot cinder, reared, and drove the saddle pommel into him as he rode through the town of Mantes which he had torched while extending his dominions. He was buried in his church of St. Stephen in Caen, but in 1793, during the French Revolution, his tomb was destroyed and his bones scattered.

✧   ✧   ✧

William the Conqueror was a direct descendant of the Emperor Charlemagne, in the 12th generation. The descent is[*]:

1. Charlemagne. King of the Franks. His grandfather Charles Martel, the Hammer, saved Western Civilization from Islam by his victory over the Saracens in the decisive battle of Tours in 732. Charlemagne conquered, Christianized and united Europe and passed the empire on to his surviving son, Louis the Pious. Later it divided into present-day France, Germany and Italy, governed by Charlemagne's descendants.

   Charlemagne was crowned as the first Holy Roman Emperor by the Pope on Christmas day, 800. A porphyry disc, on which I have knelt, in the entrance of St. Peter's in Rome marks the coronation site, and an

---

[*] H.M. West Winter, *The Descendants of Charlemagne 800–1400* (1987).

Plantagenet Descent

equestrian statue of Charlemagne stands in the courtyard. Charlemagne, in fact and legend, is the dominant world figure in the 1,000 year span from the fall of the Roman Empire to the High Renaissance.

2. Pepin. King of Italy. Charlemagne named two of his sons Pepin in honor of his father. The first was a hunchback and therefore debarred from kingship and entered a monastery. The second was crowned King of Italy, but predeceased his father.

3. Bernard. Succeeded his father as King of Italy, but also died young.

4. Pepin. Count of Senlis, Peronne and St. Quentin.

5. Herbert I. Count of Vermandois. For four generations the line would center at Vermandois.

6. Herbert II. Count of Vermandois. His sister married Robert I, the elected King of France, thereby infusing Charlemagne's bloodline into what would in two generations become the hereditary Capetian monarchy. Robert's major accomplishment was to defeat the Northmen in 911, conclude the treaty with Rollo, their Duke, and thus settle and confine the Normans in Normandy. Herbert himself married King Robert's daughter from a previous marriage, thereby making Robert an ancestor of William the Conqueror, the most significant of all the Normans.

7. Robert of Vermandois. Count of Meaux and Troyes.

8. Adele of Vermandois. She married Geoffrey, Count of Anjou.

9. Ermengarde of Anjou. She married Conan, Duke of Brittany.

William the Conqueror

10. Judith of Brittany. She married Richard II, Duke of Normandy.
11. Robert the Devil. Duke of Normandy.
12. William the Conqueror. Duke of Normandy and King of England.

William the Conqueror's wife, Matilda, was also a direct descendant* of Charlemagne, of King Alfred the Great, and most recently, of Hugh Capet, who had been elected King of France in 987 and had established the hereditary French monarchy by having his son crowned during his lifetime.

✧ ✧ ✧

Humphrey de Bohun was one of William the Conqueror's barons who fought next to him on horseback at the Battle of Hastings**. Two centuries later, as we shall see in Chapter 8, Humphrey's descendant, Humphrey de Bohun VIII, Earl of Hereford and Essex, would marry William's descendant, Princess Elizabeth Plantagenet.

---

* Winter, *supra*, and XIII D.N.B. 49.

** Anthony J. Camp, *My Ancestors Came with the Conqueror, Those Who Did and Some of Those Who Probably Did Not* (1994).

King Henry I mourning the death of his only legitimate son in the wreck of the White Ship.

Count Geoffrey Plantagenet (enameled tomb effigy in Le Mans). At 14, he married the 25 year old Empress Matilda, daughter and heir of King Henry I.

Eleanor of Aquitaine (wife of King Henry II) and her daughter-in-law Isabella of Angoulême (wife of King John and mother of King Henry III). *Mural, c. 1200, Chapel of Saint-Radegone, Chinon, France*

invaded Normandy and, exactly 40 years after the events of 1066, the reverse conquest, of Normandy by England, was accomplished with the defeat and imprisonment for life of Duke Robert Curthose. Henry I was now King of England and Duke of Normandy.

King Henry I had long been in love with Matilda, daughter of Malcolm III King of Scotland and Saint Margaret, and great-granddaughter of the great English hero King Edmund Ironside. He proposed. The English were delighted. Here was a king, albeit Norman, who had been born in England, who spoke and read and wrote English and Latin, who was now to marry one of "England's rightly kingly kin," in the words of the Anglo-Saxon Chronicle. Three months after Henry was crowned, the wedding took place and Matilda was crowned in Westminster Abbey. He was 32 and she was 20. His example was followed by others, and intermarriages between Normans and English became common. As Alexander the Great had promoted intermarriage between Greeks and Persians, so did King Henry I encourage intermarriage to amalgamate the English and Normans within his kingdom. His efforts were so successful that he has been called the refounder of the English nation. He did his part by fathering 25 illegitimate children.[2]

King Henry and Queen Matilda had two surviving children: Matilda, born in 1102, named for her mother, and William, born in 1103, named for the Conqueror. The Conqueror may not have had any English royal blood, but these grandchildren of his were direct descendants of King Ethelred the Unready, as Edward the Confessor had been. In a brilliant dynastic move, Prince William was married to the daughter of Count Fulk of Anjou. Anjou, in the wrong hands, could be a thorn in the side of Normandy. Princess Matilda was married to the Holy Roman Emperor.

In 1118, Queen Matilda, who wore a hair shirt and spent her

King Henry I

life tending the sick, died at Westminster Palace, aged 38, and was buried in Westminster Abbey*. Then disaster struck. William, aged 17, drowned, with many young English lords and ladies and much treasure, in the foundering of the White Ship returning to England from France in 1120. Henry, aged 52, immediately took a second wife—who proved barren**. The dynasty seemed lost. No woman in a millennium had reigned in her own right over either England or Normandy. Yet all that Henry had for an heir was his daughter Matilda, married to the Holy Roman Emperor. At the age of 23, she became a widow, without children. Desperately, at the Christmas assembly at Westminster, Henry caused the prelates and barons to swear that if he died without a male heir they would receive Matilda as Queen of England and Duchess of Normandy. He then negotiated her marriage to Count Fulk's son Geoffrey Plantagenet. After five years of stormy marriage, she bore a son Henry in 1133 and a second son Geoffrey in 1134. The dynasty seemed assured.

King Henry I could die content. He did, the next year, of food poisoning, on 1 December 1135, aged 67, in Lyon, after eating a large dish of lamprey against the advice of his physician, and was buried in England in the church of the monastery he had founded at Reading. The dynasty was assured.

---

* Her father, King Malcolm III of Scotland, had killed the usurper, Shakespeare's Macbeth, in battle in 1057 and himself had died in battle opposing William Rufus in 1093, when she was 13.

** Ironically, after Henry's death she re-married and had seven children (Weir, p. 48).

Chapter 3

Geoffrey Plantagenet* Count of Anjou (1113–1151)
m. 1128
Matilda the Empress (1102–1167)

Matilda was born in London in 1102, the daughter of King Henry I of England and Queen Matilda, daughter of the King of Scotland. Her paternal grandfather was William the Conqueror, who could trace his ancestry back to Charlemagne. Her maternal great-great-great-grandfather was King Ethelred the Unready, who could trace his ancestry back to King Alfred the Great, and who was the father of King Edmund Ironside and his half-brother King Edward the Confessor. English royal and Normandy ducal blood ran in her veins.

Her younger brother William was the heir apparent to the English throne and the Normandy duchy, but had drowned at the age of 17 in the foundering of the White Ship in 1120. Her first husband, the German King and Holy Roman Emperor, Henry V, to whom she was betrothed when she was eight and married when she was 12 and he was 33, died after 11 years of marriage, when she was 23, leaving her childless. Her father had plans for her and brought her back to England. She was now the heir presumptive to the English throne, and the prelates and barons swore an oath of fealty to her, a woman, at Christmas 1126 at Westminster. Her father then caused her to be married to Geof-

---

* See footnote p. vii.

frey Plantagenet, son of the Count of Anjou, on 17 June 1128. She was 25 and he was 14—32 years younger than her first husband. A son, Henry, was born to them five years later. For a third time the prelates and barons swore fealty to her and this time to her son as well. On 1 December 1135 her father King Henry I died. Now, at the age of 33, she would mount the throne.

Instead, England chose her cousin Stephen for its ruler, and Normandy followed suit. Both England and Normandy broke their oaths to her, to her father King Henry I, and to her son Henry. Both chose a man over a woman. Both chose Stephen, son of King Henry's sister Adele, over Henry's own daughter.

Matilda chose war and almost pulled it off. She invaded England, and at one point had Stephen in chains before her. But her imperious and haughty ways drove supporters away. The moment passed forever.

It was a different story on the continent. By force of arms Geoffrey in 1144 conquered Normandy for her, and in 1150 she and Geoffrey ceded the duchy to their 17 year old son Henry. Geoffrey died on 7 September 1151, aged 38, and was buried in the cathedral at Le Mans. Matilda died on 10 September 1167, aged 65, choosing to be buried in the abbey church of Bec. Centuries later her remains were reinterred in the cathedral church of Rouen. Graven on her tomb is the epitaph: "Here lies Henry's daughter, wife and mother; great by birth—greater by marriage—but greatest by motherhood." We now turn our attention to her son.

King Henry II disputing with Becket, before 1170.

Chapter 4

King Henry II (1133–1189)
m. 1152
Eleanor of Aquitaine (1122–1204)

King Henry II was born in Le Mans, Anjou, France, on 5 March 1133, the eldest son of Geoffrey Plantagenet Count of Anjou and Matilda daughter of Henry I King of England and Duke of Normandy. Although both England and Normandy had sworn fealty to his mother and to him, both opted for his mother's cousin Stephen upon the death of Henry's grandfather when Henry was only two.

Henry's father conquered Normandy for Henry's mother, and in 1150 when Henry was only 17 they ceded it to him. In 1151 when Henry was only 18 his father died and he inherited Anjou. In 1152 when he was only 19 and she was 30 he married Eleanor of Aquitaine and took control of the Duchy of Aquitaine. In 1153 when he was only 20 he went to war with his cousin Stephen of England. All the heart and fight had gone out of Stephen with the recent deaths of his wife and eldest son, and after nine months of battle Stephen recognized Henry as his successor. In 1154 when Henry was only 21 Stephen died. This was an unprecedented five years of acquisition. At 21 Henry was master of England and of most of France.

Personally, Henry II was a lion, with matted tawny hair, a freckled muzzle and boundless restless energy. He was king. And after 19 years of chaos, England was a jungle. Henry began to set things straight. He was one of the two great medieval English Kings (his great-grandson Edward I would be the other). He surrounded himself with men of genius. In 1166 his edicts from Clarendon re-made the English judicial system: they set forth a code of laws, as distinct from a mere re-assertion of "custom"; they subordinated the overlapping feudal tribunals to one uniform judicial administration; they "established once for all, so far as England was concerned, the old Teutonic principle of the right and the duty of a people to govern itself, in its own courts and by its own customary procedure, as against the Roman law which was fast taking its place in continental Europe; and it opened an almost boundless field for the training of the English people in self-government, by bringing home to every man his share in the administration of justice and police."[3]

About the same time Henry established the writ of "novel disseisin" that enabled any man dispossessed of his property without legal warrant to claim reinstatement from the king. Hereforth, every man's home was his castle. This was the greatest event in the history of English law.

In the greatest success lies the greatest failure. Thomas from Becket, Henry's closest friend, with a genius for administration, had helped Henry transform the bureaucracy, the courts and the church. To accomplish the final reformation of the church, Henry made Thomas Archbishop of Canterbury. The appointment transformed Thomas rather than the church. Thomas became a complete reactionary, upholding every anachronistic right of the church, such as the exemption of priests from prosecution for felonies. Henry's destruction of the obstructionist Becket helped destroy Henry. Yet, for as long as he lived, Henry kept improving the laws and the administration of justice in England.

King Henry II

Henry II, as noted, had married Eleanor, Duchess of Aquitaine, in 1152, when she was 30 and he was 19. They had four sons who reached maturity: Henry (1155–1183); Richard Lionheart, born at Beaumont Palace, Oxford on 8 September 1157; Geoffrey (1158–1186); and John (Henry's favorite), born at Beaumont Palace, Oxford on 24 December 1167. Together with Queen Eleanor the four sons opposed Henry, and each other, at every turn*. Part of the problem was that King Henry II had by Eleanor more sons than kingdoms. Finally they destroyed Henry.

Henry II died in France on 6 July 1189, aged 56, and is buried in the Abbey at Fontevraud in Anjou. Eleanor died on 1 April 1204, aged 82, and is also buried at Fontevraud. King Richard Lionheart, who succeeded his father, reigned for 10 years (1189–1199), and spent only six months of his 10 year reign in England. He also is buried in the Abbey at Fontevraud. Upon Richard's death his younger brother John, who lacked land, became King of England in 1199.

---

* Henry's relations with Eleanor and his legitimate children were not improved by the fact that he had 12 illegitimate children, including four by Alice, daughter of Louis VII, King of France, while she was betrothed to Henry's son Richard Lionheart (Weir, p. 63).

King John's effigy in Worcester Cathedral

Chapter 5

King John "Lackland"* (1167–1216)
m. 1200
Isabella of Angoulême (c. 1187–1246)

King John was born on 24 December 1167 at Beaumont Palace, Oxford, the youngest son of Henry II King of England Duke of Normandy Count of Anjou and Eleanor of Aquitaine. On the death of his brother King Richard Lionheart in 1199, John became King of England. His life was marked by two signal failures and no successes. Before 1215 he lost Normandy, Brittany, Anjou, Maine and Touraine to France, and in 1215 he was forced by his barons to sign Magna Carta**. The latter failure was however of inestimable value to the common people as well as to the barons. Magna Carta provides universal rights. It states:

> John, by the grace of God King of England . . . to his archbishops, bishops, abbotts, earls, barons . . . and all

---
* John was a living illustration of the New Testament parable of the talents. John was nicknamed "Lackland" by his father King Henry II because John, as the fourth son, had not been given any land. Much family bitterness and actual warfare was caused by King Henry II's efforts to reallocate lands from John's three elder brothers to John. When John finally succeeded to the throne at the age of 32 after the death of his three elder brothers, he proceeded to lose most of England's French possessions as well as much of England itself.

** As we shall see in Chapter 8, Henry de Bohun, Earl of Hereford, was one of the 25 barons who were guarantors of Magna Carta.

Plantagenet Descent

his faithful subjects, greeting. Know ye that we ... have by this our present Charter confirmed, for us and our heirs forever:

We grant to all the freemen of our kingdom, all the below-writ liberties (clause 2)

No scutage or aid shall be imposed ... unless by the general council of our kingdom [no taxation without representation] (clause 12)

Nothing henceforth shall be given or taken for a writ of inquisition ... but it shall be given freely [the writ of habeus corpus] (clause 36)

No freeman shall be taken or imprisoned, or disseized, or outlawed, or exiled, or in any way destroyed, nor will we go upon him, nor will we send upon him, except by the lawful judgment of his peers or by the law of the land [trial by jury] (clause 39)

We will sell to no man, we will not deny to any man, either justice or right [equal protection] (clause 40)

All merchants shall have safe and secure conduct to go out of, and to come into, England, and to stay, and to pass as well by land as by water, for buying or selling, without any unjust tolls (clause 41)

All persons are to be free to come and go and stay in the land in time of peace, except outlaws, prisoners or enemy aliens (clause 42)

All the customs and liberties, which the king has promised to observe toward his men, all other men shall observe towards theirs (clause 60)

Given under our hand, in the presence of witnesses, in the meadow called Runnymede, the 15th day of June, in the 17th year of our reign.

On 24 August 1200, John had married the 13 year old Isabella of Angoulême. Their elder son Henry III was born at Winchester Castle, Hampshire, on 1 October 1207, and, surprisingly, was

King John "Lackland"

named for John's father, whom John had consistently betrayed*. John's life was one of constant misadventure, in terms of family relationships (he fought his father who adored him, and his brothers, who did not; he killed his wife's lovers—"hang[ing] her gallants over her bed"—and imprisoned her); in terms of foreign policy (he lost most of England's French possessions); and in terms of domestic policy (he lost most of England to his rebellious barons and Prince Louis of France).

John died at Newark Castle in Lincolnshire on 19 October 1216, engaged in a death struggle with his rebellious barons and Prince Louis of France. John is buried in Worcester Cathedral, where his effigy still survives, and was succeeded by his elder son King Henry III.

---

* The most poignant betrayal episode occurred when King Henry II and King Philip Augustus of France exchanged lists of their supporters for the other to pardon. John's name headed the French list. Henry II saw his son's name at the head of the list of traitors to him. He turned his face to the wall and died.

Chapter 6

King Henry III (1207–1272)
m. 1236
Eleanor of Provence (1224–1291)

King Henry III was born at Winchester Castle, Hampshire, on 1 October 1207, the elder son of King John of England and Isabella of Angoulême. He came to the throne at the age of nine when his father held only western and southwestern England and a barrier of midland castles against the rebel barons and Prince Louis of France who held London, the southeast and the north. He was crowned in the west at Gloucester Cathedral. William Marshall Earl of Pembroke became regent and reconquered England for the boy king.

King Henry III assumed control of the realm while still underage, and throughout his long reign engaged in one foolish incompetent or extravagant adventure after the other, influenced by his mother's relatives from Poitou and his wife's relatives from Provence and Savoy. Finally, bankrupted by an escapade to make his younger son king of Sicily, which adventure Henry had been suckered into by the Pope, and facing excommunication by the Pope for being unable to finance the attempt, Henry once again turned to the barons for yet more money.

This time the barons responded with demands that led to the first written constitution in English history: the Provisions of Oxford, which required that Henry govern solely on the advice of a privy council, that all officials be placed under such council, that all officials swear to obey only the joint orders of king and council, that Henry govern honestly and impartially, and that parliament meet thrice yearly (6 October, 3 February, 1 June). Furthermore, as Magna Carta had by its terms extended the barons' rights against the king to the people's rights against the barons, an undertaking was made in 1259 that all reforms enjoined upon royal officials should apply equally to baronial officers. Lastly, the Provisions of Westminster, a code of legal and administrative reforms, were drafted.

After receiving the requested taxes, Henry III had the Pope annul the Provisions; the barons restored them; Henry had Saint Louis of France appointed arbiter to annul them once again; the barons restored them once again, this time by force of arms. Finally, after Henry's eldest son, the Lord Edward, had defeated the barons at Evesham in 1265 (where Earl Humphrey de Bohun V and his son Humphrey VI fought on opposite sides and the latter died), Henry accepted the more moderate settlement of the Dictum de Kennilworth, and accepted, in slightly altered form, the Provisions of Westminster as the Statute of Marlborough. English constitutional life had been forever changed.

King Henry III had married the cultivated 12 year old Eleanor of Provence on 14 January 1236, and England had been overrun by her self-indulgent relatives. As to his virtues, part of the package was that Henry was a great patron of literature, art and architecture. He thoroughly rebuilt, really created, magnificent Westminster Abbey. England became a more beautiful and more civilized country. Henry III was an indulgent husband, a much beloved father, and even his countrymen usually referred to him as "good King Henry." Their eldest child, who would become King Edward I, was born at the Palace of Westminster in 1239, when his mother was 16. Henry III died on 16 November 1272 and is buried in Westminster Abbey, next to Edward the Confessor, but

The Palace of Edward I
(above Traitors' Gate)

The Throne of King Edward I

King Henry III

his heart was sent to the Abbey at Fontevraud where his grandfather King Henry II, his grandmother Eleanor of Aquitaine, his uncle King Richard Lionheart, and his mother are buried. Dante placed King Henry III in the valley where sit those who were careless of the great reward, but not unfruitful or evil.

King Edward I
(North Transept and Sedilia, Westminster Abbey)

Bohun

shanks," and blond, with high cheekbones and a violent temper (all four characteristics perhaps showing his Viking-Plantagenet blood).

He may have been England's greatest medieval king. His two great accomplishments were, first, following in the footsteps of his great-grandfather King Henry II, to gradually (1275–1290) supplant local, chaotic feudal law with national law, and, second, to reconstitute Parliament, in 1295, so that towns had representation along with the nobles, higher clergy, and knights. This was an essential step on the road to democracy.

He died on 7 July 1307, aged 68, at Burgh by Sands, Cumbria, while preparing once again to fight the Scots. He is buried in Westminster Abbey, next to the tombs of his wife and father, where there is a sculpture of his head in the north transept and a life-sized contemporary painting of him in the sedilia near the altar. Both show him handsome and clean shaven. Illustrations shown.

In 1993, his palace, at the Tower of London, was opened to the public for the first time ever. The palace, situated immediately above Traitors' Gate, overlooking the Thames, was restored by the Historic Royal Palaces Agency. The restoration of the only surviving medieval palace in Britain contains meticulous reproductions of Edward's throne and other furniture and fixtures.

❖   ❖   ❖

To recapitulate the last seven chapters, Edward I was the 5th Plantagenet king of England. The Plantagenets stemmed from Matilda, daughter of King Henry I of England and granddaughter of William the Conqueror, whose throne was usurped by her cousin Stephen in 1135. Matilda's second husband was Geoffrey, Count of Anjou, who customarily wore a sprig of the golden broom plant in his hat: Planta (sprig) genêt (broom plant). As a resolution of the wars between Stephen and Matilda, it was

King Edward I

agreed that Matilda's son by Geoffrey should succeed Stephen as King of England. This happened in 1154 with the succession of her son as King Henry II. There has been no break in the "English" royal bloodline from William the Conqueror to Queen Elizabeth II. Henry VII, great-great-great-grandson of Edward III, was the direct ancestor of the Tudors, the Stuarts, and the Hanoverians, the latter being Elizabeth II's line. The Plantagenets are however generally considered to comprise at most Henry II, Richard Lionheart, John Lackland, Henry III, Edward I, Edward II, Edward III, Richard II, Henry IV, Henry V, Henry VI, Edward IV, Edward V, and Richard III. Henry VII, the first "modern" king, is not grouped with the Plantagenets, although, as noted, he was the great-great-great-grandson of Edward III.

The royal coat of arms, through King Edward I, was gules three lions passant gardant in pale gold (red field, three pale gold walking lions facing viewer). (The medieval heraldic word for gold was "or" but the College of Arms now uses the word "gold.") Illustration on dustjacket.

✧　✧　✧

Edward I conquered and incorporated Wales into England. His son and successor Edward II was intentionally born in Wales and invested as the first Prince of Wales, giving the Welsh "a successor king born on Welsh soil and speaking not a word of English" or any other language at his birth.

Chapter 8

Humphrey de Bohun VIII, 4th Earl of Hereford and 3rd Earl of Essex, Constable of England (c. 1276–1322)
m. 1302
Her Royal Highness Princess Elizabeth Plantagenet (1282–1316)

Her Royal Highness Princess Elizabeth Plantagenet, 13th of 16 children of King Edward I of England and Eleanor of Castile, was born in August 1282 in Rhuddlan Castle, Flintshire, Wales, as a consequence of which she was often called "the Welshwoman." Her younger brother, later to be Edward II, was also born in Wales, two years later, and was the first English Prince of Wales.

When she was 14 she married John I, Count of Holland and Zeeland, on 18 January 1297 at Ipswich Priory Church, Suffolk. He died two years later, in 1299.

When she was 20 she married, 2d, Humphrey de Bohun on 14 November 1302 at Westminster Abbey.

They had 11 children. Her Royal Highness Princess Elizabeth died aged 34 about 5 May 1316 at Quendon, Essex, in giving birth to their 11th child, who also died. She is buried in Walden Abbey, Essex.

The founder of the de Bohun family in England was Humphrey, kinsman and companion in arms of William the Conqueror. The founder of the family fortune was a later Humphrey

Plantagenet Descent

(d. 1187) whose marriage to Margaret, the eldest daughter of the Earl of Hereford, brought vast estates and the office of Constable of England. His grandson Henry (d. 1220) was created Earl of Hereford in his own right in 1200 and was one of the 25 barons who were guarantors of Magna Carta in 1215; his marriage to Matilda, sister and heiress of the Earl of Essex, brought their son Humphrey V that additional title and vast estates in Essex. His great-grandson was the Humphrey under discussion.

Humphrey's life was spent fighting the Welsh, the Scots and his wife's brother: King Edward II. In 1310 he was one of the 21 nobles appointed to reform the government and the king's household. Edward II accepted the banishment of his favorite, Piers Gaveston, but violated the ordinances by soon recalling him. The confederate barons and earls rose in arms, defeated the king, and beheaded Gaveston. When the king took another favorite, Hugh le Despenser, the nobles rose again. In the drawn-out encounters that followed, Humphrey was killed, aged 46, opposing Edward II in the battle of Boroughbridge, Yorkshire, on 16 March 1322. He is buried in the church of the Friars Preachers of York. (Five years later, Edward II's jealous wife, Isabella of France, and her lover, Roger Mortimer, would depose Edward and kill him [with a red-hot poker up the rectum] and Hugh le Despenser. Edward III, son of Edward II and Isabella, would succeed to the throne, and in due course have Mortimer hanged.)

In 1325, Lady Margaret de Bohun, daughter of Earl Humphrey and Princess Elizabeth, was therefore an orphan aged about 11, her father having been killed when she was eight and her mother having died when she was two. King Edward II, her uncle, caused her to be married to Hugh de Courtenay, aged 22, whose father, Baron Courtenay, would become 1st Earl of Devon in 1335 and be succeeded by this son in 1340.

Earl Humphrey and Princess Elizabeth would have a great-

Humphrey de Bohun VIII

granddaugther, Lady Mary de Bohun, who would marry Henry Bolingbroke*. He became Duke of Hereford before becoming King Henry IV of England.

Princess Elizabeth—Countess of Hereford and Essex—had 15 siblings. But only she and her sister Joan—Countess of Gloucester—married English spouses. In a monumental study, the whole progeny of these two daughters of King Edward I were documented down to the 17th century. A second monumental study, *The Plantagenet Roll of the Blood Royal*, by the Marquis of Ruvigny and Raineval, published in 1911 and reprinted in 1994, reported there were between 80,000 and 100,000 living descendants of Princess Elizabeth's nephew, King Edward III. By contrast, King James I had only 1,440 living descendants.[5]

The de Bohun arms are azure a bend argent cotised gold between six lioncels also gold (blue field, a diagonal silver band between two gold stripes and six rearing gold little lions). Illustration shown.

---

* A Plantagenet great-grandson of King Edward II, called "Bolingbroke" because he was born at Bolingbroke castle, Lincolnshire.

Chapter 9

Hugh de Courtenay, 2d Earl of Devon (1303–1377)
m. 1325
Lady Margaret de Bohun (c. 1314–1391)[6]

Lady Margaret de Bohun was born about 1314, the 10th of 11 children of Humphrey de Bohun, 4th Earl of Hereford, 3d Earl of Essex, Constable of England, and Her Royal Highness Princess Elizabeth Plantagenet.

When she was about 11 she married on 11 August 1325 Hugh de Courtenay, 22, who became 2d Earl of Devon in 1340. Her dowry included Powderham Castle near Exeter in Devonshire, still the Courtenay family seat in 1994.

Hugh de Courtenay was born 12 July 1303, became Knight Banneret* in 1327, fought in France and Scotland, drove the French back from their descent on Cornwall in 1339, and succeeded to the title in 1340. His father, also named Hugh, was Baron Courtenay and, from 1335, 1st Earl of Devon. The family had been dominant in Devonshire since the 12th century.

Hugh de Courtenay and Lady Margaret de Bohun had 17 children, nine daughters and eight sons, including Lady Margaret de Courtenay, their first-born. When she was no older than five, she

---

* A Knight Banneret fought under his own banner, usually supported by a number of Knights Bachelor. A Knight Banneret was usually created in the field for valor. His superior gallantry and wealth drew other knights to his banner.

was betrothed, in 1331, to the 15 year old John de Cobham, who would become the 3d Baron Cobham. The marriage was made by the girl's grandfather, Baron Courtenay, who would be created an earl four years later, and by the boy's grandfather, the 1st Baron Cobham. At this time England had about 7 earls and 129 barons, no dukes, marquises or viscounts, and about 3,000 armigerous families.[7] The ages should not shock. "Girlhood was brief. Women were marriageable at twelve and usually married by fourteen. Heiresses might be married in form as young as five and betrothed even younger, though such unions could be annulled before consummation. By twenty a woman had a number of children, and by thirty, if she survived the hazards of childbirth, she might be widowed and remarried, or a grandmother."[8]

Hugh de Courtenay and Margaret de Bohun's fourth son, William Courtenay, c. 1342–1396, became Archbishop of Canterbury. When he was Bishop of London, he had a violent dispute on 23 February 1377 with John of Gaunt, Duke of Lancaster, son of King Edward III, over the prosecution of Wycliffe, whom John favored. John snapped at William, "Thou trustest in thy parents, who can profit thee nothing; for they shall have enough to do to defend themselves."[9] The ironies are rich, for John of Gaunt's brother was married to a de Bohun, and John's own son, the future King Henry IV, would in three years marry her sister.

Hugh died that very year, on 2 May 1377, aged 73; Margaret died on 16 December 1391, aged about 77. Their grandson, Edward, succeeded to the title as 3d Earl and became Earl Marshal. They are buried in the south transept of Exeter Cathedral where in 1993 their tomb can be viewed, as can Powderham Castle located in a large deer park eight miles S of Exeter. Courtenay monuments are in the 13th century church in Sheviock in Cornwall, five miles from Plymouth.

Hugh de Courtenay, 2d Earl of Devon

The Courtenay arms were gold three torteaux a label azure (gold field, three red globes suspended from a blue bar). Illustration shown. In the 19th century the label azure was dropped. It had been adopted in 1153, when Renaud de Courtenay came to England, with the soon-to-be King Henry II, to distinguish his arms from those of his son-in-law Pierre "de Floris" second son of King Louis Le Gros of France. Pierre had adopted the name and arms of the Courtenays when he inherited their considerable French estates on his marriage to Isabella and insisted that, being of the Blood Royal, he should be the senior Courtenay branch and his father-in-law should take the label azure as a mark of a cadet or junior branch.[10]

Charles Christopher Courtenay, born 13 July 1916, is the current and 17th Earl of Devon.

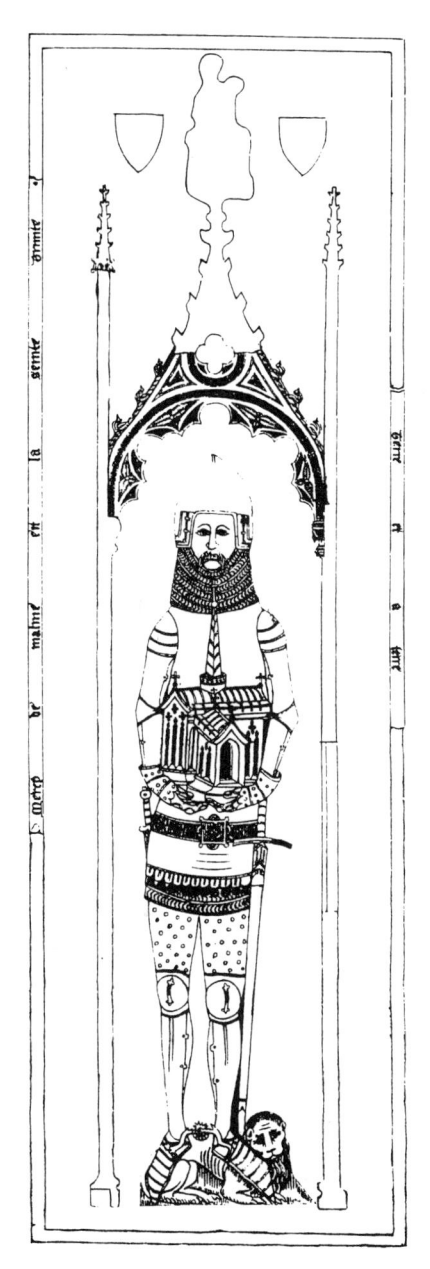

John, Lord of Cobham. ob: 1408
Cobham Church, Kent

Margaret, Lady of Cobham. ob: 1395.
Cobham Church, Kent

Chapter 10

John de Cobham 3d Baron Cobham (1316–1408)
m. 1332
Lady Margaret de Courtenay (c. 1326–1395)

John de Cobham, son and heir of John de Cobham 2d Baron Cobham and Joane Beauchamp, daughter of John 1st Lord Beauchamp of Somerset, was born in 1316 in the village of Cobham which lies 25 miles SE of Buckingham Palace.[11]

When he was 15 he was betrothed to Lady Margaret de Courtenay, the eldest of the seventeen children who would be born to Hugh de Courtenay 2d Earl of Devon and Lady Margaret de Bohun who had married on 11 August 1325.[12] The D.N.B. states, "He married Margaret, daughter of Hugh Courtenay, [2d] earl of Devonshire*, to whom he was perhaps betrothed, if not actually married, as early as 1331."[13] The Church booklet states: "Married to Lady Margaret Courtenay, daughter of the Earl of Devon in 1332." She could not have been more than five years old in 1331, her parents having married in 1325. However, her mother had been 11 when she married, and King Henry II's eldest son was only five when he married the two year old daughter of the King of France. These early marriages were of course not consummated until the girl came of age. In fact the couples often did not even live in proximity to each other. Note, too, that the time intervals

---

* The original title was "Devonshire" but "Devon" is used throughout for clarity.

Cowling Castle, in Kent.

John de Cobham 3d Baron Cobham

even out: Lady Margaret de Courtenay was betrothed (or married) in 1331–1332 but her only surviving child, a daughter, was not married until 31 years later, in 1362, indicating that Lady Margaret de Courtenay did not have this child until she was well of age, having this daughter when in her 20s.

This daughter, Lady Joane de Cobham, was named for the 3d Baron's mother.

The 3d Baron succeeded to his father's title on the latter's death on 25 February 1355. He was summoned to Parliament six months later. In 1362 he founded a chantry for five priests, which in 1993 provides housing for 13 elderly couples resident in Cobham village. He refurbished St. Mary Magdalene Church in 1367 and had his brass effigy done then. He was ambassador to France and to the Pope in Avignon and, with Geoffrey Chaucer, to Bruges in 1375. He was made a Knight Banneret in 1370, receiving 100 marks yearly pending grants of land "for the better maintenance of the estate of Bannerette." He commanded three knights, 105 esquires, 110 men at arms and 110 archers.[14] Following a disastrous raid by French and Spanish troops in 1379, he, then Warden of the Cinque Ports, obtained a license from the King to crenelate* his manor house at Cooling (Cowling). Permission to crenelate was granted by King Richard II who sent his own architect, the great Henry de Yvele, to supervise Cooling Castle, which was started in 1381 and finished in 1385. It "was probably the last genuine castle built in England."[15] Illustration shown. Cooling is 10 miles N of Cobham. In 1993 the magnificent castle still stands, in ruins, enclosing eight acres, with the Cobham arms on the 40-foot-high gate house bearing enamel plates in the form of a

---

* "To crenelate" is from the French "to indent," i.e., to create battlements behind which one could hide and shoot arrows. For obvious reasons, crenelation required the consent of the king who often was leery of his barons' fortifying their castles.

Plantagenet Descent

deed with the arms as the seal. The deed states, in Middle English, "I [the castle] am mad[e] in help of the cuntre" to protect against future raids by the French. The ruined castle walls reach a height of 10 to 40 feet in an unbroken Inner Ward stretching 196 feet by 170 feet.[16] In 1386 Lord Cobham was one of 13 lords appointed to regulate the royal court and finances, but 12 years later, in 1398, Richard II had his revenge by condemning him to death and then commuting the sentence to banishment to the Isle of Jersey for having so served, with death being the penalty for attempted escape. When Henry IV deposed Richard II in 1399, Cobham was recalled. He continued to be summoned to Parliament until he was 89.

His wife had died on 2 August 1395, aged perhaps 69; he died 10 January 1408 "in his 92nd year and was regarded as the most eminent statesman of his time."[17] He is buried in St. Mary Magdalene Church in Cobham with his wife, to both of whom there still exist in 1993 life-sized brass effigies. Illustrations shown. He is shown holding the Cobham church in his hands. The lion under his feet represents his courage; the dog at her feet represents her nobility. The death date on her brass is written MCCCLXXXXV, instead of MCCCXCV; and her father is referred to as "Counte de Devenschir" instead of "Earl," indicating the strength of Norman culture.

The Cobham arms are gules on a chevron gold three lions rampant sable (red field, on a gold chevron three rearing black lions).

✧ ✧ ✧

The family of Cobham, which took its name from the village, stems from Serlo de Cobham who owned property in the parish in the late 12th century. Cobham means village (ham) on the top (kopf) of the hill. Serlo's son Henry was a Crusader in 1191, purchased the manor of Cobham in 1208 and held the office of

John de Cobham 3d Baron Cobham

Lieutenant of Dover castle. His descendants were lawyers. His son John the Elder was Keeper of Rochester castle (a Michelin one-star in 1993), Sheriff of Kent, a Justice Itinerant and a Justice of the Common Pleas. He purchased the manors of Cooling and West Chalk in 1241. His son John the Younger followed in his father's footsteps as Sheriff and Justice, became a Baron of the Exchequer, Constable of the castle and city of Rochester, and died in 1300. He substituted 3 lions rampant sable on the Cobham arms for the previous 3 fleurs-de-lis azure. His son Henry succeeded him as Constable of the castle and city of Rochester and became Constable of the castles of Dover and Warden, fought in 1311 for Edward II in Scotland, became a Justice in the same year and custodian of the forfeited lands of the Templars in 1312. Then in 1313 Edward II summoned him to Parliament as the 1st Baron Cobham. As Constable of the castle of Rochester he received into his custody Queen Elizabeth, the captured wife of Robert Bruce, King of the Scots, whose descendants, the Dukes of Lennox and Earls of Darnley, in a knife twist of history, would, three centuries later, take permanent possession of his own Cobham estates when the then Lord Cobham opposed the ascendant Scotsman, James I, who had succeeded Elizabeth I as monarch.[18]

Returning for a moment to John Cobham the Younger, father of the 1st Baron, we can catch a fascinating glimpse of upper-class economic life in 1300. Three extant parchments from the last decade of the 13th century give us this insight, for they show that he owned 5 manors (Cooling, Cobham, West Chalk, Aldington, Beckley), comprising 2769 acres, 1793 being demesne lands and 976 being leased to 187 tenants. Of these tenants, 142 held 5 acres or less, 42 held 6 to 30 acres, one held 48 acres, one held 82 acres and one held 139 acres. At Cobham Manor alone, John Cobham the Younger owned 752 farm animals: 19 horses, 46 oxen, 6 harrowing beasts, 4 bulls (3 immature) and 23 cows, 18 rams and 87 ewes (plus 427 sheep and 58 lambs), 2 boars and 4 sows, 1 cock and 57 hens. Grains and vegetables were cash crops but the big money came—then as later—from wool. John the Younger employed, at Cobham Manor, a permanent staff of 16 and a part-time staff of 10.[19] This large agricultural base helped propel his son into the nobility. And, as we have seen, this son, having become a baron, married his 15 year old grandson to the 5 year old granddaughter of Baron Courtenay, later Earl of Devon.

Sir John de la Pole and Lady Joane de Cobham
Chrishall Church, Essex

Chapter 11

Sir John de la Pole (d. 1380)
m. 1362
Lady Joane de Cobham (d. c. 1379)

Sir John de la Pole was married to Lady Joane de Cobham in 1362, when both of them were minors.[20] They had two children, William, named for the father's father, who died without issue,[21] and Lady Joane de la Pole, who would succeed to the title of Baroness Cobham on the death of her grandfather on 10 January 1408. This daughter was born about 1379,[22] 17 years after her parents were married. Lady Joane de Cobham probably died in her 20s in giving birth to this daughter. The following year Sir John de la Pole died, also in his 20s. Since Sir John's father had married in 1351,[23] Sir John could not have been more than 29 when he died.

Sir John de la Pole was a scion of England's richest merchant family; it would be the first to make its fortune in trade and achieve a dukedom, the first dukedom not based on royal blood.

The de la Pole fortune was founded by two entrepreneurial brothers from Hull. "The relative obscurity of the brothers de la Pole makes their subsequent rise to eminence the more spectacular. Their success was achieved primarily through service to the crown, but this was made possible by the solid achievements of their early years. Their business activities . . . fall into two categories, trade and money-lending."[24] They were England's first

Plantagenet Descent

large-scale investment bankers. Both brothers lent money to, and raised money for, the crown and others.

Banking, that is, lending money at interest, was condemned by the church no matter what the interest rate. Thus the commonest method of avoiding sanctions was to discount the loan, the debtor undertaking to pay a larger amount than the loan, with no mention of interest being made. At other times bankers charged no interest and received cash "gifts." The de la Poles' effective interest rates were 22 percent; the Italian merchant princes, as foreigners less likely to collect, charged 46 percent.[25]

Sir Richard, the elder brother, was born about 1295, married "Joan" about 1313, and made his first money by importing foodstuffs during the famine of 1316. In 1317 he and his younger brother, Sir William, were made deputies of King Edward II's butler in Hull. As such, he levied an import duty on wine and also had the right to buy wine for the King's use at the fixed rate of a penny a gallon, some of which might be diverted. He was made collector of customs for the port of Hull, the largest port in England, and "gauger of wines throughout the realm." In 1322, after King Edward II had defeated the Barons, and slain Humphrey de Bohun Earl of Hereford, Sir Richard purchased their forfeited goods. In 1326, he was made deputy "keeper" of Hull, which had been a royal town since its purchase by King Edward I in 1293 from the monks of Meaux. In 1327, already wealthy, he became "butler"* to the 15 year old King Edward III and the next year left Hull for London to be nearer the center of power. He died

---

* He was not the only royal "butler" who prospered. "Henry III's butler, a knight named Poyntz Piper, enriched himself as a member of the king's household 'by unlawful as well as lawful means,' according to Matthew Paris, progressing from the ownership of a few acres of land to 'having the wealth of an earl.'" A butler (or bottler) was in charge of the buttery where beverages (wine, ale, beer) were kept, in butts or bottles. Gies, pp. 104, 96.

Sir John de la Pole

in 1345, having invested heavily in real estate. His elder surviving son, Sir William (the younger) (1315–1366), named for Sir Richard's brother, served in Parliament in 1339, married Margaret Peverel in 1351, and became a country squire, owning, among many other properties, Castle Ashby, 5 miles E of Northampton, which his wife had inherited. In 1362, while preparing to go on a pilgrimage to the Holy Land, Sir William (the younger) arranged to marry his only child, his minor son, (Sir) John de la Pole, to the only child, the minor daughter, of John de Cobham 3d Baron Cobham.

In the meantime, Sir Richard's younger brother, Sir William, for whom Sir Richard had named his heir, rose to even greater heights. Sir William had also lent money to the crown and in return had become collector of customs in London and other principal ports and engaged massively in the wool trade. He became the first mayor of Hull, an M.P., and Edward III's chief financial agent. At the beginning of the Hundred Years War he lent Edward III more than £100,000 in 1338–39; in 1339 he was made 2d baron of the exchequer and created Knight Banneret, generally awarded for gallantry on the battlefield. He was granted a monopoly of the wool export trade in 1343. Despite setbacks, his wealth continued to grow. His son Michael became 1st Earl of Suffolk, and Michael's grandson became the 1st Duke of Suffolk. The family was the richest merchant family in all of England.

Meanwhile, in 1362, in connection with his planned pilgrimage, Sir William (the younger) negotiated the marriage of his heir apparent to the presumptive heiress of a peer: Lady Joane de Cobham, infant daughter of the 3d Baron Cobham and his wife Margaret de Courtenay, daughter of the 2d Earl of Devon. The child was, as noted, Lord Cobham's presumptive heiress and the price paid for the marriage by Sir William depended on her remaining so. If Cobham's wife Margaret (then aged about 36) died without producing a son by Cobham so that Lady Joane or her issue inherited certain of her parents' lands, Sir William would pay Lord Cobham 450 marks (£300) [over a half million dollars in 1993 purchasing power]. If Lord Cobham himself died without a son, Sir William would pay 1450 marks to Lord Cobham's executors. In any case, Sir William gave the young couple four manors and a 200 acre messuage, and Lord Cobham gave them £300 in cash. Further arrangements were made for the custody of the couple and their land until they grew up, and for what was to be done if one of them died. Each father was to keep custody of his child for two years, after which they were to live with Sir William "until his said son shall be able to rule himself."[26] That attended to, Sir William visited Pope Urban V in Avignon, who wrote on his behalf to insure safe passage to the embarkation port in Sicily.[27] Sir William did not after all go on that pilgrimage but died four years later, in 1366,[28] and Sir John as his sole heir inherited his lands.

Of the de la Poles it has been written, "No other medieval family rose so far, so fast and managed to retain its position for so long."[29]

The de la Pole arms in this branch are azure two bars wavy argent (blue field, two wavy silver bars). A collateral branch substituted gold for silver.

Sir John de la Pole and Lady Joane de Cobham lived in Chrishall in Essex and at Castle Ashby in Northampton, with their infant children, William (who died young) and Joane (who would succeed her grandfather as Baron[ess] Cobham), and with Sir John's mother, Margaret. The "lands in the town of Cristeshale" came into the hands of Sir John's father in a swap with the father's uncle William in 1353.[30] In 1993 Chrishall is a village (population 400) 10 miles south of Cambridge, with a pre-Conquest church restored and rededicated (from the Virgin Mary to the Holy Trinity) by the de la Poles in the 14th century.[31] Sadly, both Sir

Sir John de la Pole

John died and Lady Joane died in their 20s. Sir John made his will on Thursday 1 March 1380 at Castle Ashby directing that he "be buried in the church at Crysteshale between the tomb of Margaret his mother and Johanne his late wife."[32] Sir John died in 1380.[33] His death may have occurred before 29 March and certainly before 27 June. A court record dated 29 March provides for payment by the bride's family in excess of 800 marks for the marriage of "William son and heir of Sir John de la Pole," payment to be made to his grandfather "John de Cobeham lord of Cobeham in his inn in the parish of St. Dunstan near the Tower of London."[34] Other court records dated 27 and 28 June refer to Sir John as "deceased."[35] Since I have discovered his will of 1 March 1380 referring to his "late" wife, IV D.N.B. 612 and 11 Kent 187 are wrong in stating that she "died about 1388." (In 1388 the Prioress of Higham [near Cobham] received £35 to pray for the family, but the money probably came from the Baron.) Sir John and Lady Joane are buried in the church in Chrishall where today their 14th century life-sized brass (illustration shown) still shows them affectionately holding hands. The brass shows her wealth by her many-buttoned dress, her nobility by her dog, and Sir John's courage by the lion under his feet. The de la Pole and Cobham arms are depicted in three shields on the brass: de la Pole, Cobham, and de la Pole impaling Cobham.

Their deaths left their infant son and one year old daughter orphaned. Their grandfather, the Baron, negotiated marriages for both of them within the year. By 1391, the daughter had borne a child and been widowed, all by the age of 12. Poor little rich girl. When she was about 13, her grandfather arranged the second of the five dynastic marriages she would make.

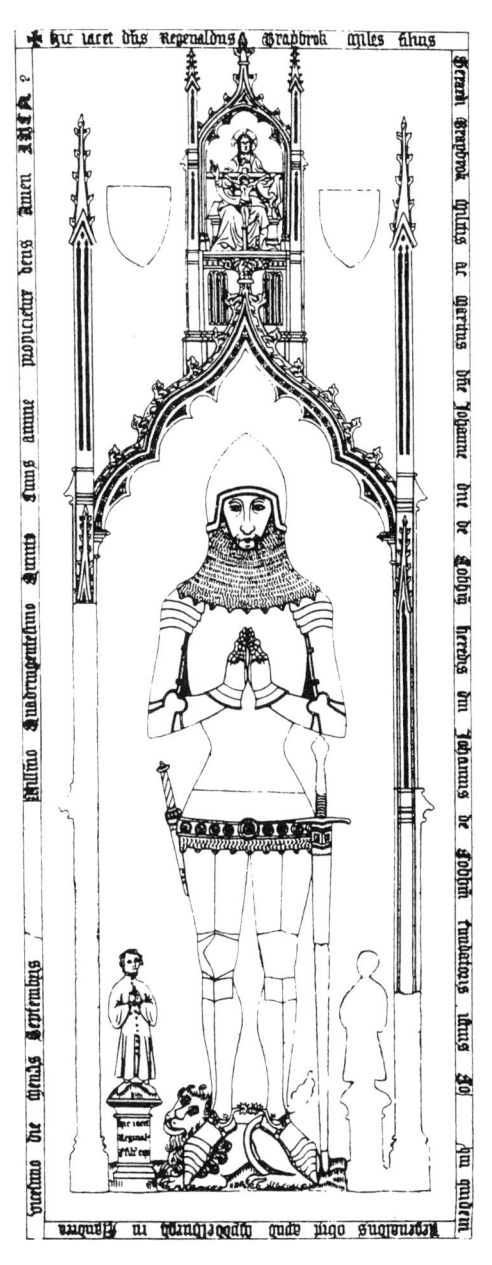

Sir Reginald Braybroke. ob: 1405
Cobham Church, Kent

Joan, Lady of Cobham. ob: 1434
Cobham Church, Kent

Chapter 12

Sir Reginald de Braybroke, Knight Banneret (d. 1405)
m. 1392
Lady Joane de la Pole (c. 1379–1434)
4th Baron(ess) Cobham in 1408

Sir Reginald de Braybroke's father was Sir Gerard de Braybroke III who married Margaret, daughter of John de Longueville,[36] and his grandfather was Sir Gerard de Braybroke II who married Alianore, daughter of Almaric de St. Amand, 3d Baron St. Amand.[37] Sir Reginald's brother was bishop of London. Had he lived long enough, Sir Reginald might have become Baron St. Amand in his own right and Baron Cobham by right of his wife. An early ancestor was Sir Henry de Braybroke, King Henry III's justice, for whose rescue the King stormed and dismantled the Earl of Bedford's castle, seat of the Beauchamp family, in 1224.[38]

Lady Joane de la Pole was born about 1379.[39] Her mother was Lady Joane de Cobham, daughter of the 3d Baron Cobham and Lady Margaret de Courtenay. Her father was Sir John de la Pole of Chrishall, Essex, of the extraordinarily wealthy merchant and (later) ducal family, son of Sir William (the younger) de la Pole and Margaret Peverel daughter of Sir John Peverel of Castle Ashby, Northamptonshire.

During her first year of life, three epic events happen to Joane. Her mother died, probably in giving birth to her in 1379 (her father's will of 1 March 1380 refers to his "late" wife). Her father

Plantagenet Descent

died in 1380, probably before 29 March.[40] She was married, through the agency of her grandfather Baron Cobham (grandfather de la Pole having died before she was born) to Sir Robert Hemenhale of Norfolk "before November 1380."[41] In 1381 there was conveyed to "Robert son of Ralph de Hemenhale knight and Joan daughter of John de la Pool knight his wife . . . the manor of Brunham" in Norfolk.[42] In 1391 her first husband died leaving her a widow aged 12 with an infant son, William. Her first husband is buried in Westminster Abbey.[43]

No previous writer seems to have known the year of her second marriage, to Sir Reginald de Braybroke, Knight Banneret. Burke simply says "before 1395." But I have discovered in the court records for 1392 that the marriage probably occurred in 1392, after her first husband's death in 1391 and before 16 February 1392, the date on which Sir Reginald "Braybroke knight and Joan his wife, late the wife of Robert Hemenale" caused the Court of Chancery to issue an "Order [to the king's agent] to remove the king's hand and mettle no further with the manor of Brunham" since "the said Robert held that manor [jointly] with her" and "the king [Richard II] has taken the fealty of the said [Reginald]."[44]

In 1398, when she was 19, her grandfather the Baron Cobham was condemned to death in the revenge of King Richard II for Cobham's supervision of the crown a decade earlier, but the sentence was commuted to banishment to the Isle of Jersey. Also in 1398 the only child who would survive her was probably born. In 1399, with the usurpation of the crown by Henry Bolingbroke as King Henry IV, the Baron was recalled from Jersey.

On 20 September 1405 Sir Reginald was killed near Middelburg in Flanders, leaving Lady Joane, aged 26, a widow for the second time. Her son by her first marriage died young as did her two sons by Sir Reginald, Reginald and Robert, who are depicted on their father's brass effigy in Cobham church. Their daughter, Lady

Sir Reginald de Braybroke, Knight Banneret

Joane de Braybroke, born, as noted, about 1398, was about seven when Sir Reginald was killed. Sir Reginald's jousting helmet is in the Tower of London and is valued at £75,000.[45] In a bit of familial piety, both his and his wife's brass refer to him as dominus (Lord), although he did not live long enough to enjoy his wife's title. He was killed in 1405; she succeeded in 1408. This is perhaps an indication that his daughter commissioned his brass as well as his wife's.

The year following the death of Sir Reginald, Baron Cobham arranged the third dynastic marriage for his granddaughter who had inherited her father's fortune* and would soon inherit the Baron's lands and title: to Sir Nicholas Hawberk—who died within the year, on 9 October 1407, at the Cobham's Cooling Castle. His well-preserved brass in the Cobham church, St. Mary Magdalene, is the "finest military brass of the period."[46] and he was a renowned tournament jouster. By Sir Nicholas she had a son, John, who died as an infant.

Thus, in 1408, Lady Joane, aged 29, was wealthy, thrice married, thrice widowed, an orphan, who had already had five children, only one of whom would survive her. Her grandfather the Baron was 92. On 10 January 1408 he died, and she became the 4th Baron(ess) Cobham.

Now that she was a baroness, the King himself would find or at least have a say in the choice of her husband. What better choice could King Henry IV make than his son Prince Hal's close friend, Sir John Oldcastle, who had fought in the wars, sat in

---

* In 1380, the same year that he had caused Lady Joane to be wed to Sir Robert Hemendale, grandfather Cobham also negotiated the marriage of Lady Joane's brother William. Court of Chancery, Close Rolls 1377–1381, p. 370. We do not know whether William died before that marriage was finalized, but we know that he died young causing his sister to be their father's heir.

Plantagenet Descent

Commons, and was now a widower for the second time. Oldcastle was probably born in 1378,[47] so he would have been 30 and Joane 29 when they wed. King Henry IV was 43 and Prince Hal was 22.

So, before the year was out, she was wed, "before 18 July 1408," for the fourth time, to Sir John Oldcastle, and became an actress on the larger stage of history, which role ended nine years later, with his execution. But first, Oldcastle, in the right of his wife, *jure uxoris*, was called to Parliament as Lord Cobham, on 26 October 1409. Now he was sitting as a lord, not as a knight. He continued to be called to Parliament through 22 March 1413.

Oldcastle had adopted Lollard opinions before 1410, when the churches of Hoo, Halstow and Cooling on Joane's estates in Kent were laid under interdict for the unlicensed preaching of "Sir John [Lay] the Chaplain." Oldcastle, as noted, was an intimate of Prince Hal, had fought under his command in 1403 when the Prince was only 16, and held high command from him in France in 1411. In one of the ironies of history, Oldcastle would become, in the hands of dramatists, the dissolute boon companion of the dissolute Prince Hal. In truth, neither was dissolute, and the defamation arose in part from a temporary dispute Prince Hal had with his father in 1411, and in part from an effort to blacken the Lollards. Shakespeare, nearly two centuries later, in reworking this material, would, in deference to the then Lord Cobham, change the name of the character in his manuscript from Sir John Oldcastle to Sir John Falstaff when *Henry IV* was printed in 1598. The greatest irony is that Oldcastle was in fact a valiant soldier and a religious reformer, of sober mien. As noted, he was a follower of Wycliffe, and would become a leader of the Lollard radicals. His relations with the ecclesiastical hierarchy were accordingly not good. In the convocation that assembled at St. Paul's on 6 March 1413, shortly before the death of Henry IV on 20 March, Oldcastle was accused of heresy. But his friendship

Sir Reginald de Braybroke, Knight Banneret

with the new king, Henry V, prevented any decisive action against him. In fact Henry V summoned him to Parliament on 22 March 1413. Then Lollard tracts were found in a book he owned, discovered in a shop in Paternoster Row. Refusing to recant, he was convicted as a heretic on 25 September 1413. Henry granted a respite of 40 days in the hope of saving the life of his old friend who, during that respite, escaped from the Tower. Finally, in late 1417, Oldcastle, who had been a fugitive and revolutionary since his escape, was captured and summarily executed on Christmas Day by hanging and burning "gallows and all." He and the Baroness had at least one child, a daughter, Joane, who died young. The barony, at least in parliamentary terms, lay dormant from Oldcastle's death in 1417 until revived in 1445.

After Oldcastle's execution, the Baroness married, for the fifth time, "before 1428," Sir John Harpenden, who died in 1458.[48] He is buried in Westminster Abbey. She died on 13 January 1434, aged 55, and is buried in the family church, St. Mary Magdalene, Cobham, Kent, England, where in 1993 there still exist life-sized brass figures of her and Sir Reginald de Braybroke. Illustrations shown. In all, she had six sons and five daughters, the six sons and four daughters who predeceased her being depicted on her funeral brass. We do not know the names of two of the sons nor three of the daughters, all five of whom may have died at birth, and were probably children by Oldcastle and Harpenden. The six children whose names we do know are mentioned above.

Illustrations of the life-sized funeral brass effigies of Sir Reginald de Braybroke and Baroness Joane de Cobham begin this chapter. Six coats of arms surround her effigy. They are:

> Upper left: Cobham; Upper right: Cobham impaling Courtenay, representing her mother through grandfather Cobham and grandmother Courtenay; Middle left: Peverel and de la Pole quartered impaling Cobham, representing her father through grandmother Peverel

Plantagenet Descent

and grandfather de la Pole; Middle right: quartered Cobham and de la Pole, representing herself; Lower left: Braybroke impaling Cobham, representing her husband and herself; Lower right: Brooke impaling Cobham, representing her son-in-law and daughter.[49] Peverel is in the first quarter of their shield showing that the Peverels had been armigerous longer and more importantly than the de la Poles.

The Cobham arms are gules on a chevron gold three lions rampant sable (red field, on a gold chevron three rearing black lions); Courtenay, gold three torteaux a label azure (gold field, three red globes suspended from a blue bar); Peverel, gules fess argent between six crosslets flory gold (red field, silver bar separating three gold expanded-end crosses above and three below); de la Pole, azure two bars wavy argent (blue field, two wavy silver bars); Braybroke, argent seven mascles 3, 3 and 1 gules (silver field, seven hollow red diamonds, configured 3, 3, 1); Brooke, gules on a chevron argent a lion rampant sable crowned gold (red field, on a silver chevron a rearing black lion crowned in gold).

Chapter 13

Sir Thomas Brooke (c. 1392–1439)

m. 1410

Lady Joane de Braybroke (c. 1398–1442)

5th Baron(ess) Cobham in 1434

The Brookes had long been established in Somerset. Sir Thomas Broke lived at Brooke Manor near Ilchester (near Yeovil) in the 14th century.[50]

His son and heir, also Sir Thomas Broke, married before 1392 "Iohane [Joane] Hanape of Co. Gloucester, widow of Robert Cheddar of Bristol."[51] He owned at least five manors—Holditch (adjoining Thorncombe), Hotham, Cherd, Cotteleygh, and Wyercrofte. In 1410 he caused his 18 year old son, also Sir Thomas Brook, to be married to the presumptive heiress of the 4th Baron (ess) Cobham. The marriage contract, dated 20 February 1410[52] was signed by him and by Lord John Oldcastle and the Baroness Cobham (step-father and mother of the bride).[53] This second Sir Thomas Broke executed his "wille . . . in my Manour of Holdech[54] on Setrynsday in . . . MCCCCXV." Text of will shown.[55] Unlike many knights, Sir Thomas Broke could write, and he dated his will with several flourishes in his own hand and concluded: "Thys twey [twain] Lynis I wrete almeste with myn own Hond." He died three years later in January 1418.[56] His will gives a fascinating look at religion, charity and property in 1415. He gave a fortune to his poorest tenants and to the blind and lame and advised his executors to actually make such distributions under threat of

The two following wills, of Sir Thomas Broke, the father, and Sir Thomas Broke, "lord of Cobham," the son, are from Furnivall, pp. 26–28 and 129–130.

THOMAS BROKE, Landowner, of Holditch, Thorncombe, Devonshire, 1417.*

[To be buried in Thorncombe Church, under a plain flat stone; not in a coffin, but only a cloth; and no feast to be held. But 300 Poor to be fed, and have 3*d*. each, and 300 Children 1*d*. Poor tenants to have £20 among em; the poorest tenant**£100; and £10 and more to go as restitution for wrong-doing. £100 to poor Blind and Lame. Residue to Wife.]

(March, leaf 316, back, Prerog. Court.)

In the name of the Lorde of all Lordes, the allmyȝty ymmortal Trinite, I, wrichyd Synner, Thomas Broke, in gode Mynde, and out of Sekenesse, make my testament, ȝyf it be the will of god, in this maner, prayng him, of his hye yndelesse mercy, fouchesafe to receyue my wreched vnclene soule in-to, his mercy, and kepe hyt fram dampnacion, for the meke passyoun and deth that his debonure sonne, oure lord Ihesu Crist, Soffred on the Crosse for Cherite & pety of mankynd. And my wyll is, that my body be Beryed in the Chirchhey of the Paryshchurch of Thornecombe, as men goth ouer

*New Style 1418.
**tenants.

74

in-to þe churcħ at þe Souþ Syde, ryȝte as they mowe stappe on
me / and a flat᷎ playne stone, saue my name ygraued þar᷎-In, that
men mowe the rather᷎ haue mynde on me, and pray for me. And
nether᷎ wheche , ne leede, to be leyde in / bote a grete Clothe to hely
my foule Caryin ; and of Torches, bote .iij., and .iij. taprys ; Ande
no fest᷎ noþer terment᷎ yholdᷓ, bot .iij., Masses atte my buryyng᷎,
saue CCC poure men schullen haue mete & drynke ynowe, and
euery man and woman of ham .iij.. dᷓ, & euery chyldᷓ of .CCC.
Childerne .I. [dᷓ], yf þer be so many Childerne / and .xiij. poure men
clothedᷓ in Russett ylynedᷓ witt white, and euery of ham to haue
.viij dᷓ / and I bequethe to my poure tenauntes of Holdycħ, Hotham,
Cherd , Cotteleygħ , & Wycrofte , that haueth yȝeue to me Capouns &
bederpes and Plouwys, ȝouȝe þey be nouȝte my tenauntes, I wiħ þat
myn executours do her᷎ gre by god discrecion atte þe value of xx ħ
amonge hame / and if any oþer man or woman be, that Cane Pleyne
hym þat icħ ħaue oppressedᷓ hym), or do wrange to him, oþer yete
with my bestys his Corne oþer his grase, and nouȝte amendit hit to
hym) ; to amende sucħ trespasses, I bequethe x. ħ. : and I bequethe to
aħ my pourest tenauntes, where þat þey be, excepte ham þat I haue
ynemnedᷓ in þis bok to-for, C. ħ in mony / and I bequethe to Poure
men blynd and lame .C. ħ, and to sum trew man, by good discrecyon)
to do party the mony forscydᷓ / and namelycħ iff ycħ ħaue do wronge
to eny of my tenauntes   or mys tak hir goodᷓ, I wiħ þat it be restoredᷓ
to ham, whether᷎ it be Man or woman, be 'avysement᷎ of myn)
Executours, as þey wiħ aunswere to-for godᷓ at þe dome / and þe
resyduwe of aħ my goodys and Cateħ, in this my testament᷎ nouȝte

bequethede, ych ȝeue Holelych, and bequethe, to Iohane my wyfe, reseruynge alweys to me volle power to chaunge þis testament, oþer to mak hit more, oþer to ameñusy hit, oþer to vndo hit all, as ofte as me Lusteth, or whanne þat me lyketh, duryng my Lyfe. and to do good and trewe execucion of þis my testament, ych ordeyne and mak myne Executours, Iohane my wyfe, William Brerdon, sir Iohn Dey, parsone of Bageworthe, Raufe Perceuale, sir Edward Osbourne, vicary of Thornecombe. This testament is my volle & hole wille þe day of þe date of þis my testament, the date in my Manour of Holdech, on Setrysday in þe vygyle of þe Holy Trynyte, the ȝere of grace & of þe incarnacyoun of oure Lorde Ihesu Criste, M¹, CCCC.ᵐᵒ xv°. Thys twey Lynis I wrete almeste with myn owne Hond.

Probatum fuit hoc testamentum coram Magistro Iohanne Estcourt &c. v°. die Februarij, anno domini Millesimo CCCC .xvij°* &c', & commissa administracio bonorum domino Edward Osbourne, vicario ecclesie parochiane de Thornecombe &c'. Reseruata potestate &c. & habent diem ad exhibendum Inuentarium primo die iuridico post sanctum Pasche proximum in futuro &c', & subsequenter acquietancia fuit dicto executori &c'.

---

*New Style 5 February 1418.

SIR THOS. BROOK, KNIGHT, OF COBHAM, 1438-9.

[To be buried in Thorncomb Church; 13 poor men to hold a torch each at the Obit; all poor blind or lame folk there to have 4*d*. each, and other needy ones 1*d*. Wife to defend Testator's Servants from prosecution by his Children and others. Residue to Wife, for herself and the true Servants, and to marry Testator's unmarrid Children with.]

(Luffenam, lf. 217, bk.)

Testamentum Thome Brook, militis.

In the name of the Fadyr & of the sonne & of the holy goost, so be hit now & evyr! the xij day of Februare, the ȝere fro the Incarnacion of our lord ihesu cryst M° cccc^{mo} xxxviij°. I. Thomas Brook, knyȝte & lord of Cobham, beyng yn hole mynde & goode witte, make my testament in this wyse. Fyrste I by-seche the most blessid Trinyte to haue mercy on me, And that thorow the prayer of the blessid Virgyne Marye, the moder of oure lord ihesu cryst, & of all the sayntys that ben in hevyn, that I, wrechid synner, myȝt the rather to haue grace worthily to be-wayle my synnys or that my sowle departe owte of this world, so that hit may be fownde clene & worthy, thorow trwe repentaunce & contynuall for-thenkyng, to be resseuyd in to the blysse that euyr shall last. More-ouer hit is my will that my body be buryd yn the north yle of the chirch of Thornecoumbe. And that at tho day of my buryng ther be saide iij masses, And all-so that þer be xij pore men clothid in white, holdyng' eche of hem a torghe brennyng' at the dirige & at the masse yn the day of my obyte. And afterward the torgis to be dalt .iij. of hem to the Chirch of Thornecombe, & the remaynande of the torgis to x of the nedyest paryschirches yn the Cuntre by sidys. Alſ-so it is my wiH that euery pore blynde, or lame man or woman that cummyth to myne obite, haue iiij ᵈ. Alſ-so it is my wiH þat euery pore nedy man, woman or child that cummyth to my obyte haue .I.ᵈ Alſ-so it is my wiH that euery man or woman that commyth home to Holdyche yn the day of my obyte after the masse is do at Thornecumbe, that thay haue sufficiante mete & drynke. Alſ-so hit is my wyH, that if þer be eny of myne owne childryn, or eny other man, that wiH trouble, disese, or pursew of my trew seruandys, & yn speciaH, Iohn Battiscoumbe, WiH Tavern or Iohn Corbrigge, that my wyff, with alle the lordeshipe and frendshipe that she may gete, socour hem, helpe hem, & defende hem, from the malice of myne owne children & of aH oþer, whiles she hath eny gode wherwith to withstande her* IvyH wyH. Alſ-so hit is my wiH that Clowys haue v. mark. And the residue of aH my godys that be not be-qwedyt yn this my testament, I ȝeue and by-qweth to my wyf, to helpe hir with, & my trwe seruandys a-foresaide, And aH-so to helpe for to mary my children that ben noȝt maryd. And that this my testament may truly be executyd, I make and ordeyne my wyfe myn executrice / and yf she wiH, Edward my sone, sir Iankyn Byschope with hir /

    Probatum fuit.   [*In margin*] acquietati sunt vere.

*their

Divine Retribution since "myn Executours . . . wille aunswere to god at ye dome [doom]." He and his wife have a brass effigy in the church at Thorncombe where they are buried. "Medieval brasses are few [in Dorset] . . . Thorncombe [has] one to Sir Thomas Brook and his wife (1419 and 1437)."[57]

The third Sir Thomas Brook was the son and heir of the second Sir Thomas Broke and was born about 1392. As noted above, he married Lady Joane de Braybroke in 1410. He was about 18 and Lady Joane was about 12 when they wed. Since the 4th Baron(ess), her mother, was only about 31, and married for the fourth time, there was no assurance that this daughter would ever succeed to the title, and indeed she did not for 24 years. He sat as a member of Parliament for Somerset from 1417 to 1427. While his wife did become the 5th Baron(ess) Cobham in 1434, he was not called to Parliament in her right as Lord Cobham. He made his will on 12 February 1439 in which he styles himself "Thomas Brook, kny3te & lord of Cobham."[58] He died in 1439, aged 47, and pursuant to his specific instructions, he is buried at Thorncombe, where he has a monumental inscription.

Lady Joane de Braybroke was born about 1398. Her father, Sir Reginald de Braybroke, Knight Banneret, was killed near Middelburg in Flanders on 20 September 1405 when she was about seven. Her two brothers, Reginald and Robert, died young and are depicted on their father's funeral brass effigy in Cobham church. As noted, she married in 1410. She lived in Brooke and Holditch while her husband served as a member of Parliament for Somerset from 1417 to 1427. They had 10 sons and four daughters.[59] She became the 5th Baron(ess) Cobham on her mother's death on 13 January 1434, whereupon she also inherited her mother's estates in and near Cobham and Chrishall. Her husband died in 1439, she in 1442. But she and her husband have no funeral brasses in the Cobham or the Chrishall church. He is buried at his testamentary request in Thorncombe, with his father. One assumes she, dying three years after her husband, is buried with her husband. It was they, however, who commissioned her mother's funeral brass in the Cobham church as is shown by the coat of arms in the lower right thereof: the Brooke arms impaling Cobham, representing the son-in-law and daughter. His will, referred to earlier, is intriguing. He spells his name "Brook." His father and grandfather spelled it "Broke." As noted, he called himself "Thomas Brook, kny3te & lord of Cobham." He says "hit is my will that my body be buryd yn the north yle of the chirch of Thornecoumbe," that there be "iii masses" and that his body be attended by "xiii pore men clothid in white" holding torches, that every poor person who attends his funeral be given a penny (three pence if blind or lame) and that those who come to Holditch after the funeral be given "sufficiante mete and drynke." He bequeaths the 13 torches to various churches. The residue of his estate he gives to his wife "to helpe hir" and "to helpe for to mary my [unmarried] children." She and "Edward my [eldest] sone" are named executors. He instructs his wife to protect his servants against the "Ivyll wyll" of their children.

The baroness died 25 November 1442, aged 44. Her oldest son, Sir Edward Brooke, had sat in Commons for Somerset in 1442, and then, following her death, was summoned to the Lords on 13 January 1445 as the 6th Baron Cobham by King Henry VI. Her younger son, Reginald Brooke, named for her father and brother, married Anne Evelyn and settled in Aspall, Suffolk, near Debenham.

The Brooke arms are gules on a chevron argent a lion rampant sable crowned gold (red field, on a silver chevron a rearing black lion crowned in gold).

Chapter 14

Reginald Brooke, Esq. (b. c. 1420)
younger brother of Sir Edward Brooke
the 6th Baron Cobham
m.
Anne Evelyn

Reginald Brooke, Esq. was a younger son of Sir Thomas Brooke (c. 1392–1439), M.P. for Somerset (1417–1427), and Lady Joane de Braybroke, 5th Baron(ess) Cobham (c. 1398–1442), who became Baroness in 1434.

His oldest brother was Sir Edward Brooke who became the 6th Baron Cobham on 25 November 1442. Both sons were probably born in the 1420s. Their parents had married in 1410.

In 1439 their father died, aged 47, having made his will on 12 February 1439. The will strangely seeks to protect his servants from his children and urges his wife to protect his servants "with alle the lordeshipe and frendshipe that she may gete." On 25 November 1442 their mother died, aged 44, while Sir Edward was sitting in Commons for Somerset, and he thereupon became the 6th Baron Cobham. About the same time he married Elizabeth, daughter of James Touchet, 5th Baron Audley. About 1444 they had their first son, Sir John Brooke (who became in due course the 7th Baron Cobham and eventually was buried and had a funeral brass, now lost, in the Cobham church). Sir Edward was summoned to the House of Lords on 13 January 1445 as the 6th Baron

Plantagenet Descent

Cobham by King Henry VI*. Sometime thereafter, however, he became an ardent Yorkist in the Wars of the Roses, and participated in the Yorkist victory at St. Albans on 23 May 1455,[60] which inaugurated the civil war. His father-in-law led the opposite (Lancaster) side for King Henry VI and was slain by the Yorkists at the Battle of Blore Heath on 23 September 1459.

---

* He might also have been the 4th Baron St. Amand. Upon the death of the 3d Baron St. Amand, Knight of the Bath, in 1403, that title fell into abeyance because Lord St. Amand left two (equal) heirs: (1) Sir Edward's great-great-grandfather (Sir Gerard de Braybroke II) who was the son of Lord St. Amand's deceased elder daughter and (2) a second daughter (by a second marriage). King Henry VI revived the title in 1449 in favor of Elizabeth de Braybroke (Sir Edward's great-aunt), whose husband, Sir William de Beauchamp, was summoned to Parliament as the 4th Baron St. Amand, by right of his wife. Burke, Dormant Peerages, pp. 464*, 32.

Sir Edward, through his deceased grandfather, Sir Reginald de Braybroke, had a superior claim to the title of Baron St. Amand, but in 1449 he had already been sitting in Parliament for four years as Baron Cobham. The St. Amand lands had been distributed, and another title without land was not worth much to him. Perhaps Sir William de Beauchamp was a political ally, either to Sir Edward or to King Henry VI. Perhaps, alternatively, Sir Edward abstained from asserting his claim for the same principle of noblesse oblige that led the English lord in the movie "Chariots of Fire" to abstain from an Olympics race, having already won a gold medal, so that someone else could win one.

The Crown can, in any case, terminate an abeyance at any time in favor of any one of the co-heirs (Debrett's, p. 61), and King Henry VI, having summoned Sir Edward Brooke to Parliament on 13 January 1445 as the 6th Baron Cobham (Burke's Peerage, p. 591), summoned Sir Edward's great-uncle, William de Beauchamp, to Parliament in 1449 as the 4th Baron St. Amand. Burke, Dormant Peerages, pp. 434*, 32. For whatever reason, Sir Edward would fight against King Henry VI in the Wars of the Roses, which would begin in 1455.

As a further irony, Sir Edward's grandson became the heir of Richard de Beauchamp, his cousin. The Brasses, p. 7.

Reginald Brooke, Esq.

Nevertheless, the triumphant magnanimous golden-haired 19-year-old Yorkist king, Edward IV, would summon his son, John Touchet, to Parliament in 1461 as the 6th Baron Audley.[61] First, however, Lord Cobham would command the left wing of the Yorkshiremen in the Yorkist victory at Northampton on 10 July 1460. Lord Cobham paid a price for his support of the Yorkist cause. The Earl of Wiltshire, a Lancasterian, with 200 men, attacked and plundered Lord Cobham's manor at Holditch, and later had Lord Cobham and his brother Peter indicted for felony.[62] The felony charges were doubtless dropped with the accession of Edward IV. Lord Cobham's parliamentary career as a lord extended from 13 January 1445 to 28 February 1463. He died on 6 June 1464, aged about 44. His wife remarried within the year without license.[63] His descendants would continue as the Lords Cobham into the 20th century (with a 300-year attainder and abeyance from 1603 to 1916 and an abeyance again since 1951).[64]

Lord Cobham's younger brother, Reginald Brooke, Esq., named for his mother's father and brother, married Anne Evelyn, and settled in Aspall, Suffolk, near Debenham. As late as 1952 his Brooke descendants were living 15 miles away, in Ufford Place, Suffolk.[65]

Through their daughter, Elizabeth Brooke, who married Francis Peyton, Reginald Brooke, Esq. and his wife Anne Evelyn were ancestors of Anne Peyton and Thomas R. Moore and Queen Elizabeth II.

Margaret Francis

Chapter 15

Francis Peyton, Esq.
m.
Elizabeth Brooke

Francis Peyton, Esq., of Bury St. Edmunds, Suffolk, married Elizabeth Brooke of Aspall, Suffolk in the 15th century. Five hundred years later, in 1993, the population of Bury St. Edmunds would be about 30,000, and the population of Aspall would be so small as not to appear even on most small-scale maps. They are about 20 miles from each other.

The Peytons had lived in co. Suffolk, in Isleham or nearby Bury St. Edmunds, for at least six generations when Francis Peyton, Esq. married Elizabeth Brooke.

The College of Arms in London indicates that John de Peyton of Suffolk was granted arms in the reign of King Edward II (1307–1327), which were still being borne by his descendant Christopher Peyton in 1612 (see Chapter 17 for a description). The earliest of his descendants (probably his grandson) listed by Paget is John Peyton (d. 1403) who married Joane Sutton, daughter of Sir Hamon Sutton, of the famous wool merchant family.[66] Their son was John Peyton who married Grace Burgoyne, daughter of John Burgoyne of Drayton. Their son was Thomas Peyton (14 February 1418–30 July 1484) who married, 1st, Margaret Bernard, and, 2d, Margaret Francis, daughter and co-heiress of Sir Hugh Francis of Gifford's Hall, Wickham Brook. Thomas Peyton

85

Plantagenet Descent

had a son by his first marriage and two sons, Crystofer and Francis, by his second marriage. This youngest son, Francis Peyton, married Elizabeth Brooke.

Elizabeth Brooke was the daughter of Reginald Brooke and Anne Evelyn. Elizabeth Brooke's uncle was Sir Edward Brooke, the 6th Baron Cobham, and her first cousin was Sir John Brooke, the 7th Baron Cobham, who was summoned to Parliament, distinguished himself in arms in the reigns of Edward IV and Henry VII, married, produced the 8th Baron Cobham, died in 1506,[67] and is buried and had a (now missing) funeral brass in the Cobham church, together with his wife.

Francis Peyton, Esq. and Elizabeth Brooke had a son, Christopher Peyton, Esq., named for the father's brother. The brother continued their father's work of altering and heightening the church at Isleham, 10 miles NW of Bury St. Edmunds, where their father Thomas Peyton and his two wives (Margaret Bernard and Margaret Francis) are depicted in 3-foot funeral brasses, he in armor, and his wives in butterfly head-dresses and wearing the same necklace*. The inscription refers to him as "armiger," one entitled to a coat of arms. Margaret Bernard brought into the Peyton family the Bernard estates at Isleham and the Mallery estates in Welton. Her dress is the more elaborate of the two.

---

* As noted in the Dramatis Personae, I have a magnificent brass rubbing made 20 years ago of Thomas Peyton and Margaret Francis and their inscription. Illustration of Margaret Francis begins this chapter.

Moulsham Hall, as built by Thomas Mildmay.

Thomas Mildmay, Auditor of the Court of Augmentations.

Sir Walter Mildmay, Chancellor of the Exchequer to Queen Elizabeth.

Sir Francis Walsingham (uncle of Christopher Peyton, Auditor General, and of Sir Richard Cooke) with Queen Elizabeth I.

Chapter 16

Christopher Peyton, Esq.
m.
Joanne Mildmay

Christopher Peyton, Esq. was of Bury St. Edmunds, Suffolk. His parents were Francis Peyton, Esq. and Elizabeth Brooke. He married Joanne Mildmay, of Chelmsford, Essex, daughter of Thomas Mildmay, Esq. (d. 1551) and Agnes Read (d. 1557), both armigerous.[68]

Joanne Mildmay had five brothers (Edward, Sir Thomas, William, John, Sir Walter) and one sister (Margery). Sir Thomas (d. 1566) was Auditor of the Court of Augmentations and of the Duchy of Cornwall at the time of the suppression of the monasteries and made a large fortune. On 23 July 1540 the family purchased from King Henry VIII the 1300 acre, 200 tenant, Moulsham Hall, near Chelmsford, where they erected a fine and famous mansion, illustration shown, which Queen Elizabeth I visited. Sir Thomas was the progenitor of Benjamin Mildmay, Earl Fitzwalter.

Joanne's youngest brother, Sir Walter, born in 1520, was the star of the family. In 1540 he was a governmental protege of his brother Thomas; in 1546 he married Mary Walsingham, the 20 year old sister of the 14 year old Francis Walsingham. Sir Walter became a brilliant Chancellor of the Exchequer under Queen Elizabeth I, and founded Emmanuel College at Cambridge University. Sir Walter was a confidant of the Queen, of Sir Francis Walsingham (who was his brother-in-law and executor), and of Sir William Cecil, Lord Burghley. Sir Walter died in 1589, leaving an estate of "at least £20,000" ($20 million in 1994 purchasing power); his granddaughter married the Earl of Westmoreland.

Christopher Peyton, Esq. and Joanne Mildmay had six children (Thomas, named for her father and older brother; Christopher, Henry, Mary, Martha, Frances). Their second son, Christopher, the subject of Chapter 17, would become Auditor General in Ireland, with the help of his uncles, Sir Walter Mildmay and Sir Francis Walsingham.

✧ ✧ ✧

Sir Francis Walsingham is one of the towering figures of world history. Born in 1530, the only son of William Walsingham, a prominent London lawyer and officeholder, Francis was raised as a zealous Protestant. At the accession of the Catholic Queen, Bloody Mary, Francis, educated at Cambridge and Gray's Inn, fled to the continent where he studied law and languages for five years, becoming the greatest linguist of his time. His father had died when he was an infant. His stepfather, Sir John Carey, was related to Elizabeth. Upon the accession of Elizabeth when she was 25 and he was 28, Francis returned to England and entered Parliament and government service, soon becoming a protege of Lord Burghley. For 40 years Burghley and Walsingham were Elizabeth's chief advisors. As noted, Walsingham's sister, Mary, married Sir Walter Mildmay, Elizabeth's Chancellor of the Exchequer.

Walsingham at the age of 32 married the daughter of the Lord Mayor of London. After her death he married, at the age of 37, Ursula St. Barbe, whose sister Margaret married William Cooke. Their son Sir Richard Cooke is the subject of Chapter 18. Walsingham was elected to Parliament throughout his career, became Principal Secretary of State in 1573 and was knighted and made

Christopher Peyton, Esq.

Chancellor of the Order of the Garter. Among his diplomatic postings as Ambassador was one to Paris where during the St. Bartholomew's Day Massacre he gave refuge to the 17-year-old Philip Sidney (about whom more momentarily) and one to the Netherlands with Lord Cobham (whose ancestors figure prominently in earlier chapters).

Walsingham's significance today stems from the fact that the intelligence service of unparalleled excellence that he created thwarted assassination attempt after assassination attempt on the life of Queen Elizabeth, thus ensuring the flourishing of the English Renaissance, which in turn led to the modern Anglo-American world of today. Walsingham's intelligence network was also instrumental in destroying the Spanish Armada when it threatened to invade and benight England in 1588.

Walsingham had no sons, which is why, unlike William Cecil, Lord Burghley, he was never made a Lord. By his second wife he did have a daughter, his namesake Frances, a great beauty* who at the age of 14 married England's most glittering prize, the dazzling courtier, soldier and poet Sir Philip Sidney, who had taken refuge in Paris with her father and her a decade earlier. Three years after their marriage, Sir Philip quixotically rode into battle in Holland against the Spanish after discarding his cuisses because a fellow knight lacked such protection. He was struck in his unprotected thigh by a Spanish bullet. Bleeding profusely and parched with thirst, he called for drink. A canteen was brought but as he raised it to his lips he saw a dying soldier and handed it to him with the words, "Thy necessity is yet greater than mine."

---

* She and Penelope Devereux (sister of the 2d Earl of Essex, lover of Sir Philip Sidney and Lord Mountjoy, wife of Lord Rich) were reputedly the two most beautiful women of the Elizabethan Age. A delightfully evocative, if historically inaccurate, novel is Jan Westcott's *The Walsingham Woman*.

Within the month he died from his wound, and England entered an unprecedented and prolonged period of mourning. For months it was considered a sin for any gentlemen to wear bright apparel in London.

Walsingham died in 1590, crushed by the burdens of office, the Queen's parsimony to him, and the staggering debts of his deceased son-in-law for whom he had stood surety, while Sir Philip Sidney's brother, who inherited most of his property, refused to contribute to the discharge of his debts. To spare his own estate the expenses of an elaborate funeral and to forestall his creditors from seizing his body, Walsingham directed in his will that he should "be buried without any such extraordinary ceremonies as usually appertain to a man serving in his place, in respect to the greatness of his debts and the mean state he left his wife and heir in." Accordingly, he was buried at 10 pm the next night, albeit in St. Paul's, in the same tomb as Sir Philip Sidney.

Later the same year, Walsingham's daughter Frances, now 20, secretly married the Queen's favorite, the 23-year-old Robin Devereux, 2d Earl of Essex, England's handsomest and richest Lord. When Frances's pregnancy revealed their secret, an enraged Elizabeth decreed that "his Countess is forbidden to show her face at court, and we command that she shall not share his dwelling spaces." The decree was never rescinded, and the Earl lived in Essex House and his Countess in Walsingham House. A son, Robert, was soon born, who would become the 3d Earl of Essex, and four other children, including a daughter, Frances, who would become an ancestress of Queen Elizabeth II.

During the decade of the 90s, the Privy Council split into two factions, one headed by Essex and the other by the Cecils. In 1599 Essex pulled the coup and tragedy of his life: he persuaded Elizabeth to appoint him Lord Deputy of Ireland. He sailed with 16,000 foot and 1,300 horse to crush the Irish rebel, the half-

Christopher Peyton, Esq.

English Earl of Tyrone, who had already destroyed one English army from ambush in the Battle of Yellow Ford. Elizabeth demanded victory; Tyrone refused pitched battles and slowly ate away at Essex's army; finally Essex concluded a secret treaty with Tyrone and, in defiance of Elizabeth's direct command, left his army to rush back to England to explain his actions to the Queen. She was not amused. Essex was imprisoned and upon his release he sought to rally London to arms against his enemies. The Queen regarded this as treason and Essex was executed.

Two years after the execution, Frances married, in early 1603, Richard de Burgh, 4th Earl of Clanricard, who, serving under Essex's replacement in Ireland, had helped defeat Tyrone and then served as governor of the de Burghs' ancestral Connaught, one of the four provinces of Ireland. Ulick de Burgh, their only son, born in London in 1604, became Marquis of Clanricard and governor of the town and county of Galway in Connaught, where he held vast estates. His annual revenues from Ireland were equal to $29 million in 1994 purchasing power.

As we shall see in detail in the next two chapters, Christopher Peyton, Esq. and Sir Richard Cooke, both proteges of their uncle Sir Francis Walsingham, also held high government office in Ireland, Peyton assuming his post with Walsingham's direct help six years before Walsingham's death and Cooke four years after Walsingham died. While Sir Francis Walsingham had no male heirs, the name "Walsingham" has been kept alive in the Cooke and Moore lines for 400 years, beginning with Sir Richard Cooke's naming his firstborn "Walsingham."

Christopher Peyton

The Armorial Bearings of
SIR RICHARD COOKE,
Knight, Principal Secretary of State in Ireland and there Chancellor of the Exchequer, granted 20 July 1612.

College of Arms
London

Lancaster Herald

Chalice in St. Werburgh's Church, Dublin, in 1993. Created by William Cooke, Esq. in 1641.

Sacheverell

Chapter 17

Christopher Peyton, Esq.
Auditor General in Ireland (c. 1544–1612)
m. 2d
Alice Newman

Christopher Peyton, Esq., of Bury St. Edmunds, Suffolk, was the second son of Christopher Peyton, Esq. and Joanne Mildmay, and a nephew of Sir Walter Mildmay, Queen Elizabeth's brilliant Chancellor of the Exchequer, who was married to the sister of Sir Francis Walsingham, Elizabeth's Principal Secretary of State.

Christopher was born about 1544 and entered government service about 1564, probably under the patronage of his uncle, Sir Walter.

In December 1581 Lord Burghley received a letter from Dublin Castle, from Auditor Thomas Jenyson, desiring that Christopher Peyton replace Jenyson as Auditor.[69] In October 1584, while in Ireland making a study of escheated lands for Lord Burghley, Christopher wrote to him, and to his two uncles, Sir Walter Mildmay and Sir Francis Walsingham, stating, "Jenyson is willing to let [me] have his office from Michaelmas last, for £600."[70] On 24 November 1585 there issued in Latin the "Grant to Christopher Peyton of the office of Auditor at Wars in Ireland."[71]

Christopher married, 1st, Anne Palmer, who probably died about 1574, leaving him a son and three daughters. He married, 2d, Alice Newman, about 1575, by whom he had a daughter,

Plantagenet Descent

Anne. Anne must have been about nine, and apparently accompanied him, when he went to Ireland in 1584. In 1589 he wrote to Lord Burghley from Dublin, stating that he had "sent, for the relief of his son, to one Monsieur Treleboys, near Rochelle, where his son is at board, certain barrels of butter, beef, candles and tallow, about a ton in all, and a small cask of apparel, intending after a time to place his son with the King of Navarre*" but that the goods were seized [by officials] for the Queen's use and praying Lord Burghley for relief.[72]

In 1595, Christopher may have married for the third time, about the time his daughter Anne married Richard Cooke. The Calendar for 10 July 1595 cryptically proclaimed: "Mr. Auditor Peyton has married Might's widow."[73] Christopher's funeral certificate would not countenance this.

In 1597 Christopher bemoaned to Lord Burghley that his "property of Rathecoole, but six miles from Dublin [1993 population 3,000], was pillaged by the soldiers and burnt by the rebels—whereby my poore towne lyeth wast and unmanured" and prayed Burghley for relief.[74] Earlier, Christopher had inhabited, among other dwellings, "the castle and lands of Mucrus court in the great county of Limerick."[75]

In July 1600 Christopher wrote to Sir Robert Cecil, Elizabeth's "prime" minister since the death of Lord Burghley two years earlier, reminding him that while the two of them were not well acquainted, he had loyally served Lord Burghley [Cecil's father] and Sir Walter Mildmay [Christopher's uncle] and the crown "for these later sixteen years employed wholly in the Irish services, and formerly twenty years together employed in England."[76]

---

* A Huguenot who within a year also became king of France as Henry IV.

Christopher Peyton, Esq.

From 1602 through 1611 Christopher's salary as Auditor was £256 15s. 0d,[77] annual raises not being fashionable in the 17th century.

On 22 May 1611 the inheritable title of baronet was first conferred, on 18 persons by King James I, one of whom was Christopher's Isleham cousin, Sir John Peyton.[78]

Christopher's funeral certificate, in the College of Arms in London, states, "Christopher Peyton, Auditor at Wars and of the Revenue, deceased the 30th Octs 1612, his former wife [Anne Palmer][79] and only son died before his comeing in Ireland; Elizabeth & Cicilie his elder daurs live in England [in 1612]; Thomasin his t'red daur was wife first to Captn Peter Baptist als Castilion; secondly to Sir Robt Pigote of Disert Knt. Auditor Peyton's wife now widow is Alis Newman by whom he left issue Anne wife to Sir Richard Cooke Knt Principal Secretary." The arms of Peyton impaling Newman are shown in a black and white shield above his funeral certificate.

Burke and Paget and other authorities describe Christopher Peyton as "Sir." Betham does not, and in his 1611 report, Peyton does not use "Sir" but "Esq." On 14 September 1993 Lancaster Herald of the College of Arms in London wrote, "the arms [of] Christopher Peyton:—Sable a cross engrailed gold in the first quarter a mullet argent [black field, a serrated gold cross, and, in the first quarter of the field, a five-pointed silver star]. I do not find that Christopher Peyton is listed among known knights, nor does his funeral certificate indicate that he ever received a knighthood." And on 30 September 1993 Lancaster Herald further wrote, "the Arms of Christopher Peyton . . . were borne by Sir John de Peyton of Suffolk during the reign of King Edward II [1307–1327]. They therefore date back to at least the beginning of the 14th century." This Sir John de Peyton was an ancestor [probably the grandfather] of the John Peyton (d. 1403) discussed in Chapter 15.

Chapter 18

Sir Richard Cooke
Principal Secretary of State in Ireland
and Chancellor of the Exchequer (d. 1616)
m. c. 1595
Anne Peyton (c. 1576–after 1637)

Anne Peyton's father, Christopher Peyton, Esq., of Bury St. Edmunds in Suffolk, was Auditor General in Ireland and died 30 October 1612. He was born in England; through his daughter Anne Peyton and the Cooke line, the next seven generations would be born in Ireland, the next three in Canada, and the next two, including Thomas R. Moore, in the United States; through his daughter Anne Peyton and the Colley line, the next six generations would be born in Ireland, and the next six, including Prince Charles, in England.

Since Anne Peyton's father did not go to Ireland until 11 years before her marriage, she was doubtless born in England.

Anne Peyton's first husband was Sir Richard Cooke, "son and heir of William Cooke of Great Lindford in the County of Buckingham, Gentleman, descended from a family of Cooke from the County of Lincoln."[80]

William Cooke had married Margaret St. Barbe whose sister Ursula St. Barbe had in 1567 married the great Sir Francis Walsingham, 1532–1590, Principal Secretary of State to Queen Elizabeth I. So Sir Francis Walsingham became the uncle of Richard

Plantagenet Descent

Cooke. The father of the St. Barbe sisters was Henry St. Barbe of Ashington, Somerset, d. 1568, who had married Eleanor, daughter of Edward Lewknor of Kingston Bewsey, Sussex, d. 1528, who was also an ancestor of the Moore branch that became the Earls of Drogheda.[81] Viscount Sir Garret Moore of Drogheda would become brother-in-law to Anne Peyton after the death of Sir Richard Cooke in 1616, when Anne Peyton would marry Sir Henry Colley.

Anne Peyton's father became Auditor General in Ireland in 1584, and she was probably living in Ireland when Richard Cooke arrived in Dublin on 1 August 1594, but travel between Ireland and England was frequent. Only 245 English families were then living in Ireland.[82]

Richard and Anne must have married about 1595, since their first son, Sir Walsingham Cooke, named for the great Sir Francis Walsingham, had an only child born in 1620. This daughter, Elizabeth, was to marry John Parsons, Esq., younger son of Sir William Parsons Baronet and Lord Justice of Ireland. Her grandnephew was created a baron and viscount and his son was created Earl of Rosse.

On 1 August 1594, Sir William Russell, fourth son of the Earl of Bedford, had arrived in Dublin as Lord Deputy of Ireland, the highest office in Ireland under Queen Elizabeth I. He was "met by the Council, captains, mayor, and other gentlemen, to the number of 500 horse." He was accompanied by his secretary, Richard Cooke, who had apparently taken that position on or before 24 June 1594, when Sir William's Journal began, probably written by Cooke (or under his direction), who first mentions himself on 25 October 1596: "Sir George Bourchier rode to Dublin with Mr. Cooke [from the fortified camp at Rathdrome]." Ten days later "Mr. Cooke [again] sent to Dublin." And then on 24 January 1597: "Mr. Molinex [Sir Thomas Molyneux, XIII D.N.B. 584], Chancel-

Sir Richard Cooke

lor of the Exchequer, died, and my Lord [Deputy Sir William Russell] bestowed that office on Mr. Richard Cooke, his secretary." On 20 April 1597 "My Lord sent Mr. Richard Cooke, his secretary, with letters to England." On 15 May 1597 Lord Burgh arrived to replace the recalled Sir William Russell as Lord Deputy. Four days later "Mr Cooke, 'our' secretary, landed with letters from England." On 26 May 1597 Sir William Russell left Ireland, Richard Cooke stayed, and the Journal ended.[83]

By 1603, Richard Cooke, Esq., held three concurrent key positions in Ireland: Chancellor of the Exchequer, to which he had been appointed on 24 January 1597 (later also Lord Chief Baron); Principal Secretary of State (appointed in 1603); and Clerk of the Crown for the Province of Connaught.[84] His annual salaries were, respectively, £14 0s. 0d. (raised to £119 6s. 8d. by 1611); £106 13s. 4d.; and £26 13s. 4d., total of £252 13s. 4d (equivalent to $250,000 in 1994). His father-in-law, Christopher Peyton, Esq., Auditor General, received a similar salary of £256 15s. 0d.[85]

On 28 February 1603, Lord Mountjoy (Charles Blount), then Lord Deputy of Ireland, wrote to Sir Robert Cecil, Secretary of State and "prime" minister of Elizabeth's government, "Richard Cooke, Esq., Chancellor of Her Majesty's Exchequer here . . . hath been bred and trained up all his life-time in her Majesty's service, as first under [Principal Secretary of State in England] Sir Francis Walsingham [his uncle, who died in 1590] and now these nine years in her Highness' service within this realm." The occasion of this letter was dramatic. One John Delahoide, being convicted of murdering his wife, had thereby forfeited to her Majesty the manor and 400 acres of land in Dunshaghlen in the county of Meath, following which the Lord Deputy and Council had leased the property to Chancellor Cooke (for a term of 21 years at a favorable annual rental of £20) as a reward to Cooke for unmasking the corruption of the Second Baron of the Exchequer, one Patrick Sedgrave. Baron Sedgrave had tried by fraud to acquire the

Plantagenet Descent

forfeiture to the Queen for himself and had offered Cooke a spurned bribe of £1,000 [four years' salary] to forbear exposing him. The Baron was dismissed from office, fined and imprisoned.[86]

On 10 December 1603, following Elizabeth's death and James I's accession to the throne, Richard Cooke was knighted at Woodstock, England.

On 12 November 1613 Sir Richard Cooke and Sir Edward Fisher each received a grant of 1,500 Irish acres.[87] Two of Sir Richard's sons would marry two of Sir Edward's daughters. During the reigns of Elizabeth I and James I there were only 31 English families who owned land in co. Wexford, 7 of which families were headed by knights, including Sir Richard Cooke and Sir Edward Fisher, one by the Anglican bishop of Waterford.[88]

"Sir Richard Cooke and Art McDermond Kevanaghe" engaged in a serious controversy in 1614 over a massive amount of escheated* lands in the county of Wexford. It was ordered that the controversy "be decided by course of law or otherwise compromitted [arbitrated] before the lands in debate between them passed by letters patent to other [either] of them."[89] We do not know the resolution of that controversy.

Sir Richard received, somewhere in Ireland, in 1615 "arable and pasture, 2,430 acres. Wood, wherein is some good pasture, 1,020; in all 3,450." Sir Edward Fisher received "arable and pasture, 1,130; woods, wherein is some good pasture, 770; in all, 1,900."[90]

On 19 March 1616, Sir Richard received 2,000 acres of escheated lands in county Wexford, as did Sir Edward Fisher. "The

---

* "To escheat" is to "fall out," i.e., to forfeit to the crown in default of a legitimate taker. The English found that the Irish usually could not prove legal ownership of land and therefore brought legal actions to forfeit the land to the Crown, after which it was leased or sold on favorable terms to English entrepreneurs.

Sir Richard Cooke

reason why Sir Richard Cooke had 2,000 acres was his claim to so much in right of his wife; Auditor Peyton, her father [d. 1612], having acquired it by purchase or gift from the natives." Sir Edward Fisher and others also received 2,000 acres each; they "had their portions larger than the rest in respect of their extraordinary travel and expenses to bring that work to effect."[91] So, Sir Richard had at least 400 acres, plus 1,500 acres, plus 3,450 acres, plus 2,000 acres, a total of at least 7,350 acres. This is more than 11 square miles, and more than twice as much as the Lords Cobham owned (see chapter 10).

Sir Richard Cooke had a grant of arms from William Camden, Clarenceux King of Arms (for Southern England), on 20 July 1612 (College of Arms in London), nine years after he had been knighted at Woodstock, England, on 10 December 1603. The coat of arms is barry of six argent and azure in chief three annulets gules (six alternating silver and blue bars with the top third being silver and bearing three red rings), of which I have a painting from the College of Arms in London. Illustration shown.

Sir Richard Cooke died on 8 September 1616, leaving Anne Peyton with at least three children, Walsingham Cooke (named for the father's uncle, Sir Francis Walsingham), aged about 18, William Cooke (named for the father's father), aged about 16, and Peyton Cooke (named for the mother's family). Her father had died four years earlier on 30 October 1612, leaving her his co-heir.

Sometime after the death of Sir Richard Cooke on 8 September 1616, his widow, Anne Peyton, married Sir Henry Colley of Castle Carbury, Kildare, which lies 30 miles due west from Dublin. Sir Henry Colley "received large grants of land in Wexford in 1617."[92] Was this an inducement for Anne Peyton to marry him or did he receive these "large grants of land in Wexford in 1617" as a result of marrying her? He died on 6 July 1637, mentioning Anne in his will and she is stated to have survived him.[93] In 1640 Anne

Peyton's firstborn, Sir Walsingham Cooke, owned at least 3,131 acres in co. Wexford (see next chapter), and her son by her second marriage, Dudley Colley, Esq., owned 1,318 Castle acres in the Parish of Carbury, co. Kildare.[94]

The Colley family was of English origin and probably came to Ireland from Gloucestershire, settling in Ireland early in the 16th century. Robert Colley was the first of the family recorded as ensconced there. He was bailiff of Dublin in 1515 and died in 1543. His grandson, Sir Henry Colley, was knighted by Sir Henry Sidney, Lord Deputy of Ireland, in 1560, was called to the privy council, received the grant of Castle Carbury, Kildare, in 1563, and died in 1584.[95] It was his namesake great grandson whom Anne Peyton married.[96]

Anne Peyton's second husband, Sir Henry Colley of Castle Carbury, had succeeded to the castle in 1601, was knighted on 18 June 1615 and, as noted, "received large grants of land in Wexford in 1617." They had children including Dudley Colley, Esq., born about 1621.[97] Castle Carbury passed to him and on his death in 1674 to his son Henry Colley, Esq., who was the great-grandfather of the Duke of Wellington. (Henry's son would be a baron, his grandson an earl, and his great-grandson the Duke.)

During the decade of the 1590s during which Sir Richard Cooke had married Anne Peyton, or earlier, Sir Garret Moore had married Mary Colley, sister of the Sir Henry Colley whom Anne Peyton would marry after 1616. Sir Garret Moore and Mary Colley had 12 children "that came to manes estate beside many that died younge," the second of which, Sir Thomas Moore, was born in 1593, indicating that they probably married before 1590.[98] This was the third interlocking family: Cooke, Colley, and Moore.

Sir Richard Cooke and Sir Garret Moore had signed joint proclamations in 1609 and 1611. The year before Sir Richard Cooke's death in 1616, Sir Garret Moore was created Baron Moore of Mellifont on 15 February 1615.

Sir Garret Moore's father, Sir Edward Moore, had, with three brothers, come to Ireland from Benenden in Kent to make their fortunes about 1550, shortly before the beginning of Elizabeth's reign. And make their fortunes they did. By 1604 Sir Garret Moore could say that he was "paying the greatest rent to the king [James I] of any man in the kingdom." Sir Garret Moore was in October 1604 made a privy councillor, in 1609 or 1610 he was granted 1,000 acres in co. Armagh for the purpose of the Plantation of Ulster, in 1613 he represented the borough of Dungannon in Parliament, on 15 February 1615 he was created Baron Moore of Mellifont, and on 7 February 1621, Viscount Moore of Drogheda.[99] Mellifont is 4 miles W of Drogheda. After his death, Mary Colley married Viscount Wilmot of Athlone, and died in 1654.

Anne Peyton would become the great-great-great-grandmother of Richard Colley Wellesley the Marquess Wellesley; and of Arthur Wellesley the Marquess and Duke of Wellington; the great-aunt of Henry Moore, the 1st Earl of Drogheda; and the great-great-great-great-great-aunt of Charles Moore, 1st Marquess of Drogheda. Her first husband, Richard Cooke, would become a distant cousin of the latter two through Edward Lewknor, a common ancestor of both the Cookes and the Moores. Anne Peyton is a direct ancestor of Queen Elizabeth II through Anne's son Dudley Colley, Esq., of Castle Carbury, his great-great-grandson Richard Colley Wellesley the Marquess Wellesley, and his daughter Anne. The full descent is Anne Peyton; Dudley Colley; Henry Colley; Richard Colley (took surname Wellesley upon inheriting his cousin's estates) 1st Baron Mornington; Garret Wellesley 1st Earl of Mornington; Richard Colley Wellesley the Marquess Wellesley; Anne Wellesley; Charles W. F. Cavendish-Bentinck; Nina Cecilia Cavendish-Bentinck; Lady Elizabeth Bowes-Lyon; Queen Elizabeth II.[100] Prince Charles, Prince of Wales, is

Plantagenet Descent

therefore a 10th cousin of Thomas R. Moore through Anne Peyton.

❖ ❖ ❖

Three great expansions or diastoles and three great contractions or systoles of the Ascendancy took place during the 223 years the Cooke and the Moore families were present in Ireland (1594–1817).

The first great expansion or diastole of the Ascendancy began with the establishment of an Anglo-Norman ruling elite in Ireland in Wexford in 1169 under King Henry II, which reached its peak under Elizabeth I. Near the end of this period, Sir Richard Cooke arrived in Ireland, on 1 August 1594, as Secretary to Sir William Russell, Lord Deputy; in May 1597 Thomas Lord Burgh succeeded as Lord Deputy; disaster struck following Lord Burgh's death during the year.

The first contraction or systole had begun in 1595 with the rebellion of the Earl of Tyrone, Hugh O'Neill, in Ulster. It reached its crescendo on 14 August 1598, when the Earl of Tyrone inflicted a crushing defeat on the Protestant Ascendancy in the Battle of Yellow Ford on the Blackwater, Ulster, where he destroyed the English army led by his brother-in-law Marshall Sir Henry Bagenal, envenomed by his sister's elopement with Tyrone. The efforts of the Earl of Essex, Elizabeth's favorite, in 1599 were unavailing. Then in 1600 Lord Mountjoy (Charles Blount) succeeded Essex as Lord Deputy and arrived in Ireland with 13,000 English troops. At about the same time, Sir George Carew was appointed President of Munster. On Christmas Eve, 1601, these combined Anglo-Irish forces met the native Irish of the Earl of Tyrone and his Spanish allies in the battle of Kinsale in southern Munster. Kinsale is near the sea, and Tyrone's forces were fighting in the open under conditions far less favorable to their special skills than the bogs and woods around Yellow Ford. Ty-

Sir Richard Cooke

rone was repulsed, and his forces scattered in disorder. Years of negotiations took place, including meetings at Mellifont with Sir Garret Moore and Lord Mountjoy, and later with Sir Arthur Chichester who became lord deputy in 1605. In 1607 the Earl of Tyrone and his ally at Kinsale, the Earl of Tyrconnel, fled Ireland forever in what history knows as the Flight of the Earls, leaving their land holdings, and those of their followers, in Ulster up for grabs.

The second diastole or expansion of the Protestant Ascendancy therefore began in 1608 with the Plantation of Ulster under King James I. In May 1610 Sir Richard Cooke was appointed a member of the Commission for passing escheated lands in Ulster to British undertakers. Sir Garret Moore received 1,000 such acres. This period of expansion continued until 1641, when the second systole, as we shall see, took the life of Sir Garret Moore's son and successor, Sir Charles Moore 2d Viscount Moore of Drogheda, and perhaps the life of Sir Richard Cooke's son, William Cooke, Esq.

Looking back on Sir Richard Cooke's life, one is bemused to recall that he combined in himself in Ireland the two offices his uncles had held in England: Sir Francis Walsingham (who married Sir Richard's mother's sister) had been Principal Secretary of State, and Sir Walter Mildmay (who married Sir Francis Walsingham's sister) had been Chancellor of the Exchequer. As noted in Chapter 17, Sir Richard's father-in-law, Auditor Peyton, was also a nephew of both Sir Walter and Sir Francis.

Chapter 19

William Cooke, Esq.
First Master of the Dublin Goldsmiths' Company
(c. 1600–1642)
m. c. 1625
Lettice Fisher

William Cooke, Esq., the second son of Sir Richard Cooke and Anne Peyton, was born about 1600. He married Lettice Fisher, daughter of Sir Edward Fisher of fashionable Fishamble Street, St. John's Parish, Dublin, and Fisher's Prospect (Courtown), co. Wexford, who was knighted in the first year of the reign of King James I at St. Mary's Abbey, Dublin, on 2 October 1603[101] (two months before Richard Cooke was knighted in Woodstock, England). Sir Edward Fisher, kt., was the highest "cessed" (taxed) parishioner of the Church of St. John the Evangelist, Dublin, paying xxs (20 shillings) in the assessment of xxvi ffebr 1621.[102] He died in December 1632, leaving five daughters.

Englishmen born in England were favored over Englishmen born in Ireland, who were favored over Irishmen. Yet Sir Edward Fisher did well, despite being in this second class, as would the Duke of Wellington two centuries later. Wellington would deny being Irish, saying, "Being born in a barn doesn't make a man a horse." Fisher, like Wellington, an Englishman born in Ireland, rose from being a lieutenant, and courier for Sir William Russell, Lord Deputy, and the Earl of Essex in 1597, to being a captain in

Plantagenet Descent

charge of 100 men as part of the contingent of 2,000 sent into Munster in July 1601, to being knighted in 1603, to receiving a "pension" from the king of £194 13s. 4d. in 1604, to judging 61,000 escheated acres in Wexford in 1611, to being granted at least 6,900 acres in 1612–1616, to being the trusted aide of Sir Arthur Chichester (who was Lord Deputy of Ireland from 1605 to 1614 and was created Lord Chichester of Belfast in 1613). One of Fisher's daughters, Elizabeth, married Chichester's nephew. Yet as late as 1602 the Privy Council wrote, "First, for Captain Fisher, although we have not heard any ill of him, yet we hold this place [constable of a fort] not fit for him, and the rather for that he is of Irish birth," and later in the same year, "place Captain Fysher [as] his vice-constable, which may be as well tolerated in him as in other Englishmen's sons born in Ireland."[103]

Sir Edward Fisher's parents were Henry Fisher, Esq., and Katherine Giggins (d. 15 October 1620). Both were armigerous, the Fishers since at least 1502.[104] Sir Edward's arms are "argent, on a chevron between three demi lions rampant gules three bezants [gold coins]. Crest-a fleur-de-lis quarterly, argent and sable."[105] Burke also notes that Sir Edward was granted 1,500 acres in Courtown in 1612 and that one of his five daughters, Elizabeth, married Edward Chichester, brother of the first Earl of Donegal (created 1647), and, as noted above, nephew of Lord Deputy Sir Arthur Chichester, whose mother was a Courtenay of Powderham Castle (see Chapter 9).[106]

Both Edward Fisher and Richard Cooke were knighted in 1603, Fisher in Dublin, but Cooke, an Englishman born in England, in Woodstock, England; he later received his coat of arms from William Camden, the Clarenceux (English) King of Arms. Since two of Sir Richard's sons would marry two of Sir Edward's daughters, the combined families would own more than 14,250 acres, more than 22 square miles, while their widowed mother,

William Cooke, Esq.

Anne Peyton, would be living on the vast estate of her second husband, Sir Henry Colley, a total the size of Manhattan.

William Cooke, Esq., the middle son, married Lettice Fisher, and apparently lived his life in Dublin as a goldsmith, the First President (Master) of the Dublin Goldsmiths' Company, an Assay Master, and Churchwarden of the Church of St. John the Evangelist. Modern Irish silver dates from the charter of 1637 given by Charles I to establish the Dublin Goldsmiths' Company. That charter repeatedly lists William Cooke first and names him a Warden. The other named Wardens elected him President ("Master"). He served as President until 1640, and as Assay Master from 1638 till his death in September 1642.[107]

Of William Cooke, Esq., and his work, the following was published in 1912:

> The earliest known specimens of Dublin date-marked silver plate which have been placed on record are, as is well known . . . a chalice in Derry Cathedral marked D (1641–2).
>
> But it does not seem to have been recorded that Dublin possesses two other interesting specimens of its early date-marked plate. They are a chalice and paten, made for the Old City Church of St. John the Evangelist, and now preserved in St. Werburgh's Church. [St. Werburgh's Church is extant in 1993 and next to The Castle and Fishamble Street and the chalice and paten are still being used in the services.]
>
> Both of these pieces of plate bear the Dublin hall-mark, the date-letter C (1640–41), and the 'maker's mark' of William Cooke, the first Master of the Dublin Goldsmiths' Company. William Cooke was closely connected with St. John's Church, for he lived at Lower Blind Quay in the parish, was churchwarden in 1639

and 1640, and was buried in the church on 17 September 1642.

The paten bears no inscription; but the chalice is inscribed 'St. John the Evangelist Dublin,' and bears also, on the underside of the foot, the inscription, 'William Cooke &'. Possibly the maker's intention was to add to his own name that of his fellow-churchwarden for 1640, Clement Martyn, brewer; but for some unknown reason the inscription was never completed.

The only other recorded specimen of date-marked plate by William Cooke is the chalice in Derry Cathedral mentioned above. It was made a year later than the St. John's chalice and paten.

From an entry in the vestry-book of St. John's during the year beginning at Easter 1639, it appears that this chalice and paten were made out of older chalices, probably pre-Reformation vessels. The entry in question runs:

> for changinge the Communion cups into one, and for the case, . . . li 07 s.14 d.00

The giving of the cup to the laity necessitated chalices larger in the bowl than were in use prior to the Reformation.

It is interesting to know that Dublin possesses these specimens of the work of the first Master of the Dublin Goldsmiths' Company.—[108]

William Cooke, Esq., and Lettice Fisher had a son, Arthur Cooke, Esq., who probably was a minor at the time of his father's death in September 1642.

Sir Walsingham Cooke, older brother of William Cooke, Esq., was born shortly before 1600. On 4 February 1618, two years after the death of their father, the Crown granted Walsingham Cooke 500 acres in co. Wexford; contemporaneously his then or about to be father-in-law, Sir Edward Fisher, received 600 nearby acres,

William Cooke, Esq.

added to the 1,500 acres he had received six years earlier. By 1620 Walsingham Cooke had wed Mary Fisher, sister of the Lettice Fisher whom William Cooke would marry. In 1620 Walsingham Cooke and Mary Fisher had a daughter, Elizabeth, their only child, who was baptized on 8 June 1620 in the Church of St. John the Evangelist, Dublin, where her maternal grandfather, uncle and parents were parishioners. The following day her father received from the King "100 marks [$66,000] a year in fee-farm." On 15 July 1630 Sir Walsingham Cooke was knighted shortly after becoming High Sheriff (the Crown's chief administrative officer) of co. Wexford. Richard and Thomas Cooke, of Dunsaghlin, co. Meath, were his sureties.[109] Could Richard and Thomas have been younger brothers to Sir Walsingham Cooke in addition to William Cooke, Esq. and Peyton Cooke? "Richard" after all was the name of Sir Walsingham Cooke's father and the custom was to name the third son after the father, the first after the paternal grandfather, the second after the maternal grandfather. In Sir Walsingham Cooke's case he was instead named for his father's illustrious uncle Secretary of State Sir Francis Walsingham, his brother William Cooke, Esq., was named for their paternal grandfather, and Peyton Cooke was given the family name of their maternal grandfather. And Sir Thomas Mildmay had been an illustrious maternal forbear.

In about 1637, aged about 17, Elizabeth Cooke married John Parsons, Esq., younger son of Sir William Parsons, Baronet and Lord Justice of Ireland. Her grandnephew would be created a baron and viscount in 1681, and his son would be created Earl of Rosse.[110]

Sir Walsingham Cooke apparently lived principally when in co. Wexford in his great house at Tomduff and his father-in-law's great house at Fisher's Prospect. In 1640 his land holdings in co. Wexford included 3,131 acres in the Baronies of Gorey and Ballaghkeen in co. Wexford (a barony was about 50 square miles and a parish about 3 square miles): 440 acres in Monamolin Parish (177 years later his great-great-great-grandnephew Walsingham Moore would be living in Monamolin) which bordered "the castle of Tomduff," 500 acres in Kiltriske Parish, 930 acres (including Tomduff's 100 acres) in Killenagh Parish, another 314 acres in Killenagh Parish, another 205 acres in Killenagh Parish, 242 acres in Donoghmoore Parish, and 500 acres in Kilcormack Parish. Some of these lands were probably inherited from his father, Sir Richard Cooke, and perhaps some by his wife from her father, Sir Edward Fisher.[111]

On 15 December 1640, Sir Walsingham Cooke's wife, Mary Fisher, died; on 3 August 1641 his younger grandson, Walsingham Parsons, died; both are buried in Tomduff in a "vault mad[e] by Sir Walsingham Cooke Knight for a burial place for himself and his posterite the XXth of October 1641."[112] In September 1642 William Cooke, Esq. died and his minor son, Arthur Cooke, apparently came to Tomduff to live with Sir Walsingham Cooke.

The year after William Cooke, Esq., died, his cousin Sir Charles Moore, 2d Viscount Moore of Drogheda, was killed in battle. Sir Charles Moore had been born in 1603, succeeded his father (Viscount Sir Garret Moore) in 1627, was present in Parliament in 1634, and was active in suppressing the Great Rebellion which began in 1641. "In September [1643] he advanced against Owen O'Neill at Portlester on the Blackwater [near Drogheda] but during the engagement on the 11th he was knocked off his horse and killed by a cannonball, fired, it is said, by O'Neill."[113] With the Restoration of the Monarchy in 1660, King Charles II rewarded Viscount Sir Charles Moore's ultimate sacrifice by creating his son and heir Henry Moore as 1st Earl of Drogheda on 14 June 1661.

The Great Rebellion of 1641 was part of a four-way conflict, inflamed by religion and nationality, that engulfed the British Isles: In 1639 the Presbyterian Scots revolted against England, the

William Cooke, Esq.

King, the Anglicans, and the Catholics; in 1640 the Presbyterian English Parliament began its death struggle with the Anglican royalists; in 1641 the Catholic Irish rebelled against the Protestant Ascendancy, the King, and the English. By the end of the 1640s, the Presbyterian English Parliament, under Oliver Cromwell, was triumphant, having pacified the Scots, having subdued the Irish after ravaging Drogheda and Wexford, and having beheaded the Anglican King Charles I.

We do not know whether William Cooke, Esq., or his wife Lettice Fisher or their son Arthur Cooke, Esq., in Dublin, were affected by the Great Rebellion of 1641, although William Cooke, Esq., was buried on 17 September 1642, aged only 42. Nor do we know if Anne Peyton (alive in 1637 when her second husband died) or their son Dudley Colley, Esq., at Castle Carbury and Edenderry, both in co. Kildare, were affected. Nor do we know whether foreshadowings of the Great Rebellion occasioned the deaths in Tomduff of Sir Walsingham Cooke's wife Mary Fisher on 15 December 1640 or of his grandson Walsingham Parsons on 3 August 1641. We do know that Sir Walsingham Cooke was joint commander with Lord Esmonde "of the Forces of the County" of Wexford and that his house at Tomduff was plundered and his goods and cattle stolen by a force of rebels led by Col. Luke Birne in November 1641.[114]

A fascinating conjecture arises in the matrix of the early death at age 42 of William Cooke, Esq., in September 1642, and his elder brother's joint command with Lord Esmonde "of the Forces of the County" of Wexford against the rebels in the Great Rebellion of 1641. In December 1641, a month after Sir Walsingham Cooke's house had been plundered, Lieut. John Esmonde, nephew of joint-commander Lord Esmonde, was, with five companions, surprised by 80 rebels under the command of Capt. James Bryan. Lieut. Esmonde's horse was killed by a bullet meant for him. Whereupon Bryan and three other rebel officers also dismounted. "Bryan drew

Plantagenet Descent

his sword and strucke at the said Lieut., and he the said Bryan and Lieut. Esmonde fought together till the said Lieut. was wounded in two places of his head with two blowes the one crosse the other, and with a blow on his right arme soe as the said Lieut. never after received the perfect use thereof; and afterwardes the said Bryan was killed by one Wm Cooke that came in with the said Lieut. after that the said Lieut. was wounded [so] that he could fight no longer, being fallen to the ground." All four of the rebel officers were killed and the others fled. Months later Lieut. Esmonde was captured and "executed [by hanging] 20 August, 1642, by Walter Roche, Provost Marshall to the Rebels."[115]

Could William Cooke, Esq., have been a combatant in his brother's forces, perhaps suffering his own death in a subsequent engagement? Or been captured and executed by the rebels? We do not know the exact date of William Cooke's death but his burial on 17 September 1642 was less than a month after Lieut. Esmonde's execution by the rebels.

As noted, William Cooke's wife, Lettice Fisher was one of five daughters who were co-heirs of Sir Edward Fisher who had died in 1632. Sir Edward had owned about 7,000 acres, most of them in co. Wexford. No lands appear in the name of Lettice Fisher or her husband William Cooke, Esq. in the monumental surveys of Irish land ownership as of 1640 ordered by the Cromwellian government in the 1650s. One of the five daughters, Elizabeth Fisher Chichester, discussed above, inherited 1,500 acres at Fisher's Prospect (now Courtown) and her son John Chichester sold those lands in 1711.[116] If Lettice Fisher had sold her lands before her husband's death in 1642, perhaps to finance his gold business, their son, Arthur Cooke, Esq., would be even more dependent for land on his uncle Sir Walsingham Cooke, or on a fortunate marriage.

Sir Walsingham Cooke's daughter Elizabeth (Parsons) died in 1656, aged 36, and was buried in St. Patrick's Cathedral, Dublin.[117]

William Cooke, Esq.

This Parsons line soon ran out, succeeded by the Eustace and Tickell lines. In 1994 the head of that family is Marston Eustace Tickell, a retired English general.[118]

Chapter 20

Arthur Cooke, Esq. (c. 1625–1682)
m. c. 1655
Margaret Sacheverell

Primogeniture, the rule of law that concentrated inheritance of land, when land was wealth, in the hands of the firstborn, drove second and later borns from England to Ireland, from the Irish countryside to Dublin, and from Ireland to the New World.

Sir Walsingham Cooke inherited more than 3,000 acres; his younger brother William Cooke, Esq., inherited no acres. And while Sir Walsingham Cooke would shelter or employ his nephew, Arthur Cooke, Esq., after the death of his father (the First President of the Dublin Goldsmiths' Company) in 1642, he would be unlikely to devise land to him so long as he had a child of his own. And we know that Sir Walsingham Cooke had a daughter Elizabeth (Parsons) and one surviving grandson Arthur Parsons through whom Tomduff and other acreage would devolve. We also know that Sir Walsingham Cooke remarried. His second wife was Catherine, daughter of Christopher Rotheram. Her will was proved on 10 May 1654.

To oversee an estate of 3,000 acres with hundreds of tenant families required a large and skilled administrative staff, and since Sir Walsingham Cooke had no sons, his nephew Arthur Cooke, Esq., perhaps played a key role in administering his holdings. Arthur apparently spent considerable time in co. Wexford. He

Plantagenet Descent

married, aged about 30, in about 1655, Margaret Sacheverell, daughter and eventual co-heir, with her sister Mary Good, of William Sacheverell, Esq., "of Ballyknockane," co. Wexford, descended from the Sacheverells of Morley in Derbyshire, by way of Ulster. William Satchiverell, Protestant, was the owner in 1640 of at least 430 acres in co. Wexford, Barony of Ballaghkeen, Parish of Castle-Ellish, townlands of Balliknockan (place of the hill), Boleboy (place of the cow), Slevegran (mountain of the corn), and Castle-Ellish.[119] These lands are located SSW of Tomduff House (ESE of Enniscorthy).

Sacheverell was one of the 10 English original planters in Ulster in the early 1600s, along with six original Scots planters. William Sacheverell had been Deputy Provost Marshall of Ulster. By 1640, as noted, he owned at least 430 acres in co. Wexford. Prior to and during the Great Rebellion of 1641 he was Register in the Diocese of Ferns in co. Wexford, an office worth £40 a year, to which, "by reason of these tumultuous times," he suffered a loss of £100. He also suffered a loss of £30 from theft of his cows.[120]

William Sacheverell's lands passed to his daughters, and Arthur Cooke, Esq. is described as "of Ballyknockane, Esq."[121]

The Sacheverells were armigerous, and their arms are set out by Sir William Betham, Ulster King of Arms, as "argent on a saltire azure 5 water bouquets or"[122] (silver field, on a blue x-shaped cross 5 gold canteens). Illustration shown. With at least 215 inherited acres of land (half of his father-in-law's holdings), Arthur Cooke, Esq. could be content as a country squire.

Arthur Cooke, Esq., named his son, born about 1660, "Walsingham" Cooke, in honor of Arthur's uncle, Sir Walsingham Cooke, who had no sons, but over 3,000 acres in co. Wexford, and whose only child, Elizabeth (Parsons), had died in 1656, aged 36. Arthur died intestate in 1682, aged about 57. Administration was given to his widow, Margaret Sacheverell, on 26 October 1682.

Chapter 21

Walsingham Cooke, Esq. (c. 1660–1724)
m. 1698
Anne Bower

Walsingham Cooke, Esq., only child of Arthur Cooke, Esq., and Margaret Sacheverell, was named for his father's uncle, Sir Walsingham Cooke, who had no sons. He lived on and inherited family estates in the three townlands of Ballyknockane, "Slievenegrane alius Cookestowne," and Ballyboy, all in the Parish of Castle-Ellish, Barony of Ballaghkeen, County of Wexford, Ireland[*]. These had been lands of his mother's father, William Sacheverell, Esq., who, as noted, owned in 1640 at least 430 acres, half of which were inherited by his mother and half by her sister.

At the commencement of the Great Rebellion of 1641, the population of Ireland had been 1,448,000: 616,000 perished in the Rebellion (504,000 natives, 112,000 English settlers and troops), 40,000 went into overseas service, 100,000 were transported to the Americas. Of Ireland's 20 million acres, 11 million acres owned by Catholics were confiscated by the Cromwellian Government and apportioned to 1,300 "adventurers" who financed the war in return for prospective Irish lands and to 19,000 Protestant officers and soldiers, a quarter of whom settled, the rest

---

[*] As previously noted, "bally" means "town" or "place," "knock" means "hill," and "slievenegrane" means "mountain of the corn" in Gaelic. Both "Ballyknockane" and "Cobham" can mean the town on the hill.

Plantagenet Descent

selling their rights. Between 1652 and 1662 the Protestant share of land in Ireland thereby increased from 41 percent to 78 percent.[123] Three families whose progeny might[124] play a vital role in the following chapters came from England to Ireland in the Cromwellian settlements: 12 Moores (including two "adventurers"), three Boltons (including a major and a captain), and one Thomas Proctor, a total of 16 families[125] that would intermarry.

In February 1689, when Walsingham Cooke was about 29, Parliament voted for the joint rule of William and Mary. A month later, the deposed James II landed from France in Kinsale in southern Ireland, and soon held a parliament in Dublin. Most Protestants refused to attend, and the therefore Catholic majority passed an Act of Attainder against more than 2,400 Protestant landowners, stripping them of all their property.[126] This probably did not affect the progeny of the Cookes, Peytons, Colleys, Fishers, and Sacheverells, at least with respect to the lands they held before 1640. But query the effect on the Moores, Boltons and Proctors. It must have relieved Walsingham Cooke, and others, when King William defeated James II at the Battle of the Boyne, near Drogheda, on 1 July 1690, thereby ensuring the Protestant Ascendancy.

In 1688 England had 160 temporal lords, 26 spiritual lords, 800 baronets, 600 knights, 3,000 esquires and 12,000 gentlemen, considerably less than one percent of the population of 5,500,520.[127] The percentage in Ireland was comparable.

Eight years after the Battle of the Boyne, in 1698, Walsingham Cooke married Anne Bower.[128] From this union were born six children:

(1) William, died without issue, named for the father's grandfathers, William Cooke, Esq., First Master of the Dublin Goldsmiths' Company, and William Sacheverell, Esq.; (2) Arthur Cooke, died without issue, named

Walsingham Cooke, Esq.

for the father's father; (3) Henry Cooke, died without issue; (4) John Cooke, Esq. (m. Magdelin Redmond, Marriage Articles, dated 14 & 15 November 1740*; d. 1747); (5) Frances (m. . . . Proctor); and (6) Jane (m. John Bolton).[129]

Proctors and Boltons, who married these two Cooke daughters, would intermarry with the Moores, as we shall see in the next two chapters. As noted, these Proctors, Boltons and Moores may have come to Ireland from England in the 1650s Cromwellian settlements. No Proctor, Bolton or Moore has been found in the 1640 survey of Irish land ownership, whereas 16 families with these three surnames are listed in the 1650s Cromwellian land grants. Three Moore families, but no Proctors or Boltons, came over in the Williamite settlements.[130]

Walsingham Cooke made his will on 12 April 1723, and died on 10 March 1724, aged about 64. His will was proved at Ferns.

---

* Their daughter Anne Cooke married a Redmond cousin whose grandson was John Henry O'Byrne Redmond who on 22 September 1849 married Emelia Georgianna Manley, daughter of General Count Manley. Their son, Reginald Pius Rudolph Plantagenet Redmond, born 1851, succeeded his father in 1866 as Count of the Papal States and inherited Sleanagrane (Cookestowne), co. Wexford. John O'Hart, Irish Pedigrees (1892, 5th ed. 1976), pp. 364–366, and G.O. 178, p. 235 (1849).

Chapter 22

Frederick? Proctor[*]
m. c. 1738
Frances Cooke (c. 1713– ?)

Frances Cooke was the fifth of six children of Walsingham Cooke and Anne Bower who were married in 1698[131] in co. Wexford. Allotting 3 years between each difficult birth, her brother John, as the fourth child, would have been born about 1710. She, as the fifth child, would have been born about 1713. Only the youngest three siblings had issue: John, Frances and Jane. John married in 1740 and died in 1747. Assuming he was born in 1710, he would have been 30 when he married, 37 when he died.

Assuming Frances married at the age of 25, her marriage would have taken place about 1738. Her husband's last name was Proctor,[132] and he was employed in the Customs Service which was centered in Dublin.[133] Mr. Proctor and Frances Cooke had a daughter, Frances Proctor, named for the mother, and about 10 years later a son, Walsingham Proctor, named for the mother's father. This daughter, Frances Proctor, married William Moore, and named her second son Frederick Moore, apparently in honor of her father.

---

[*] Sir William Betham's Registered Pedigree does not give Proctor's first name. The best surmise is that it was Frederick since the tradition was to name one's second son for the mother's father and Proctor's daughter Frances Proctor who married William Moore named their second son Frederick.

Plantagenet Descent

Frances Proctor, on the above calculations, would, if born first, have been born about 1741. If she in turn was 25 when she married William Moore, she would have married in 1766, and if she had a child two years later, he would have been born in 1768.

In 1768, a son was indeed born to Frances Proctor and William Moore. This son was named "Walsingham" Moore, for the mother's brother (Walsingham Proctor) and the mother's grandfather (Walsingham Cooke). Walsingham Moore in turn gave the name "Walsingham Proctor" Moore to his oldest son born in Dublin in 1808 and the name Edward "Cooke" Howard Moore to his youngest son born in Canada in 1822. And so the wheel continues to turn.

There is reason to believe that Walsingham Proctor may have been born about 1751[134] ten years after his sister, Frances Proctor. Both he and his sister were probably born in Dublin, and surely lived there as adults.

The next chapter tells us more of the elusive Frederick? Proctor who married Frances Cooke and of the family's subsequent life in Dublin.

Chapter 23

William Moore (c. 1740–c. 1820)
m. c. 1766
Frances Proctor (c. 1741–before 1817)

Mr. Proctor who married Frances Cooke about 1738 apparently removed her from her father's house in Cookestowne, co. Wexford, to Dublin. As we have seen in the last chapter, their great-great-great-grandson told Edw. F. Moore that this Mr. Proctor, first name unknown to him, "was employed in the Customs Service," which was centered in Dublin. During the Protestant Ascendancy, the Customs Service provided a great number of lucrative jobs. As the great historian Lecky was wryly to write: "One of the . . . results of the existence of a separate Irish Parliament [which was the case until 1800] was the enormous jobbing in Government patronage, and in the dispensation of honours, that took place for the purpose of maintaining a Parliamentary majority. The Irish Custom and Revenue Departments were full of highly paid offices, which naturally entailed laborous and important duties, corresponding to those which were discharged in England by hard-working secretaries and clerks. In Ireland such posts were commonly given to members of Parliament or their relatives, who treated them as sinecures, and devoted a fraction of their salaries to paying deputies to discharge their duties."[135]

Mr. Proctor and Frances Cooke had two children, Frances Proctor and Walsingham Proctor. Each would name a child in honor of the other.

Plantagenet Descent

Walsingham Proctor, probably ten years younger than his sister, had two daughters by his first marriage: Frances Proctor born 3 June 1783, and Susannah Proctor born 1 May 1785. I have Frances Proctor's 1801 prayerbook in which she lists those names and birthdates. After the death of his first wife, Walsingham Proctor married his housekeeper, about 1811, when he was 60, to the great displeasure of his daughter Frances, then herself married for the second time and aged 28. A "Walsingham Proctor, son of Walsingham & Mary Proctor" was born in Dublin on "25 April 1814, baptised 8 May 1814," which may have been his namesake son by his second, late, marriage. A third "Walsingham Proctor, son of Walsingham & Jane Proctor of Upper Baggott Street, Dublin," probably his grandson, was born in Dublin on "12 April 1836, baptised 9 May 1836." Both births and both baptisms were recorded in the registers of St. Peter's Church (Church of Ireland, Anglican.)[136]

Frances Proctor, the older sister of Walsingham Proctor, married William Moore about 1766. The only other facts we know about William Moore prior to 1800, other than through his children, is that he is mentioned as a barber-surgeon in the Minute Books of the Dublin Guild on 14 April 1798 (see next chapter) and is listed as a "yeoman" loyalist owning property in co. Wexford which suffered damage of £10 in the Rebellion of May–June 1798. His sons signed themselves "gentlemen," i.e. members of the gentry. Royalty, peers, gentry (knights, esquires, gentlemen) and yeomen constituted the upper few percent of the populace. From 1429 to the 1832 Reform Act the term yeoman was defined in legal terms by limiting the vote to those males holding at least a "forty-shilling freehold," about 50 acres; from Elizabethan times the term yeoman was further defined economically by limiting the term to those holding at least 100 acres.[137]

William Moore and Frances Proctor had seven children: (1)

William Moore

Walsingham, b. 1768 in Dublin, admitted to the Dublin Guild of Barbers and Surgeons in 1798, married his uncle Walsingham Proctor's daughter Frances in 1805, and emigrated from Ireland to Ontario with his father in 1817; (2) Frederick, b. 1770 in Dublin, married Eliza Bolton (1773–1815) before 1794 (18 Bolton households in co. Wexford suffered property damage in the Rebellion of 1798 ranging from £10 to £2,386 [over $1,000,000 in 1993 purchasing power]); emigrated to the Township of Elizabethtown, County of Leeds, Ontario, in 1811; (3) William, who was living in Dublin in 1811, accepted a job in the Stamp Office declined by his brother Walsingham, and married Anne Dowell (probably without co. Wexford property since no Dowells suffered property damage there in 1798); (4) Daniel, b. 1781, killed at the age of 17 with 36 other loyalists near Gorey co. Wexford on "Bloody Friday," 22 June 1798, in an armed engagement, by a Catholic mob in the Rebellion of 1798;[138] (5) Elizabeth Jane (m. Samuel Rowsome who suffered damages of £38 in Co. Wexford in the Rebellion of 1798); (6) Anne, who went to Ontario with her father in 1817 and married Edward Howard there; and (7) Margaret, who went to Canada with her brother Frederick in 1811 and married and had children there.[139]

In 1783 George III created the Order of St. Patrick to consist of the sovereign, the lord lieutenant of Ireland (as grand master), and 15 knight companions. Two of William Moore's wife's distant cousins, Charles Moore, then 6th Earl of Drogheda, and Richard Colley Wellesley, then 2d Earl of Mornington, were among the 15 original knights.

In 1778 the Protestant Ascendancy created a volunteer yeomanry corps of landowners and their sons to protect against invasion by the French and the Spanish. As matters eventuated, it became crucial twenty years later, in 1798.

In 1798 there occurred one of the seminal events in the life of the Anglo-Irish Ascendancy in Ireland and in the lives of the Moore family: the adumbrated Rebellion of 1798.

In 1798 two of William Moore's wife's distant cousins, the above-mentioned Richard Colley Wellesley, then 2d Earl of Mornington, and his brother, then Major General Arthur Wellesley, were in the East, conquering and governing India for the British Empire. Nearer to home, the French were again threatening to invade Ireland to liberate it from British and Anglo-Irish Ascendancy rule.

The French Revolution of 1789 had radicalized political thinking in Ireland and elsewhere. The meaning of the French Revolution to some was that a stable society was not necessarily gridlocked and that the will of the people might be directly translated into political action. A radical society named the United Irish Society was formed in 1791 in Belfast, mostly with Presbyterian and Catholic members, to promote the unification of the disparate Catholic and Protestant Irish "nations" into one. The young Dublin Protestant Wolfe Tone was a co-founder. The Society had limited appeal. By 1796 it had gone underground and had become a secret society advocating violent means.

Wolfe Tone had in 1795 gone to France to seek revolutionary help and in December 1796 he approached the Irish coast aboard a French fleet of 43 ships and 15,000 French soldiers. The fleet tried to put ashore at Bantry in southern Munster, not far from Kinsale, where a Spanish fleet nearly 200 years earlier had landed to help the Irish rebels under the Earl of Tyrone. But the French fleet was driven off by storms. Wolfe Tone correctly remarked that England had not had such a close escape since the days of the Spanish Armada, destroyed by the intelligence gathered by Sir Francis Walsingham and English seamanship.

The near brush alarmed the government and it ruthlessly broke the secret society in its Ulster stronghold. Then, in March 1798 it arrested in Dublin the United Irish leadership which was trying to organize the society and other secret societies for a national rebellion in the expectation of a second invasion attempt by the French. The authorities found a note from a radical leader, Lord Edward Fitzgerald, indicating the port of Wexford as a possible site for the French landing.

Wexford was lightly garrisoned and the feverish job of searching for arms and information was given by the government to the local Protestant yeomanry aided by the tough Catholic North Cork militia. They did not do their job gently. On 26 May 1798, shortly after the capture of Fitzgerald's note, a local Catholic priest, Father John Murphy, led the sullen Catholic peasantry of Wexford in a local peasants revolt. The rebels won an early victory over the North Cork militia at Oulart Hill and showed no mercy to their co-religionists even though the militia pleaded for it in Gaelic, a language Wexford Protestants no longer spoke, and in English. The rebels then took the town of Enniscorthy and encamped on Vinegar Hill.

> On one side of the hill was a windmill which had a green flag planted on the top and thirty-five captured Protestants from the town of Enniscorthy stuffed inside it. The overcrowding was reduced when a dozen of them were taken out, lined up in front of the door and clumsily put to death with pikes. . . .
>
> An even more grisly revenge . . . followed a few days later when a barn holding Protestant men, women and children prisoners at a large farm house known as Scullabogue was set on fire and those not burned alive were shot or piked to death. The number of dead there may have been as many as 200.[140]

Eventually, the rebels moved north to suffer a heavy defeat at Arklow on the road to Dublin. The town of Gorey lies two-thirds of the way from Enniscorthy to Arklow, and it was at Gorey,

Plantagenet Descent

where a battle occurred, on 22 June 1798, that William Moore's 17-year-old son Daniel and 36 other loyalists were killed by the Catholic mob. William Moore's 28-year-old son Frederick also "took an active part, on the Loyalist side, in the Rebellion of '98."[141]

William Moore and his in-laws suffered damage to their properties in Co. Wexford, for which they would be compensated by the Crown in the "list of suffering loyalists*."

An adumbration of what was happening in Wexford had occurred earlier in 1798 in sporadic outbreaks elsewhere in Ireland. On 25 January 1798, for example, at what was the country estate of the Moores who are the Earls of Drogheda (Monasterevan in co. Kildare 45 miles NW of Gorey) "at four in the morning a party variously estimated at 1,000 or 2,000 attacked the little town of Monasterevan, which was garrisoned by eighty-four yeomen. There was some serious fighting, and the issue for one or two hours seemed very doubtful, but the yeomanry then drove back their assailants, who set fire to some houses and retired under the shelter of the smoke, leaving sixty or seventy of their number dead on the field. Only four or five of the yeomen appear to have fallen. It was noticed that of the gallant little band that defended Monasterevan, fourteen were Catholics, and ten others were

---

* Lists of suffering loyalists, by county, have been gathered together in the National Library, Dublin in "List of Persons Who Suffered Losses in Property 1798," (1799) JLB 94107. In Wexford, "William Moore, yeoman," suffered losses of £10. His son-in-law, "Samuel Rousome, farmer," suffered losses of £38. His daughter-in-law's family was the hardest hit; 18 Bolton households suffering damages ranging from £10 to £2,386 [over $1,000,000 in 1993 purchasing power]. For purposes of comparison, the annual wage of one of the revolutionary founders of the United Irishmen, a librarian, was £50. The losses in co. Wexford in this 6 April 1799 listing were £311,341. Musgrave, *infra*, in 1802 totals the Wexford losses as £515,191.

Methodists.... With this exception, no event of any real importance took place during the rebellion in this county."[142]

Meanwhile, back in co. Wexford, on the eve of the Rebellion of 1798, "the ... county of Wexford was ... one of the most prosperous in Ireland. Land sold there at an unusually high price. It had a considerable and intelligent resident gentry, and in general the peasantry were comfortably situated, though there were some districts in which there was extreme poverty. The people were [overwhelmingly, about 95 percent] Catholic, but mainly descended from English settlers, and this county boasted that it was the parent of the volunteer movement, the first corps [of yeomanry] having been raised [in 1778] by Wexford gentlemen."[143]

The rebellion in Wexford was effectively over in a month. It was generously estimated that 50,000 were killed, more than half in cold blood.[144] In an ironic footnote, Wolfe Tone was captured aboard a third French fleet approaching Ireland in October 1798. He unsuccessfully tried to commit suicide in his cell, but did eventually die of the self-inflicted wound.

Parliament immediately enacted legislation to compensate the "suffering loyalists" for their financial losses sustained in the Rebellion of 1798. Claims of £1,023,337 were submitted to the commissioners appointed by Parliament, over half of the claims, £515,191, being from one of the 26 counties: Wexford.[145] "The surviving sufferers made application to the commissioners appointed by parliament for part of the fund appropriated for their relief, and their loss was substantiated by their own affidavit and that of the parish minister, and was certified by their landlord and by a neighboring magistrate. Such affidavits were numerically registered in the archives of the house of commons."[146]

During the Rebellion of 1798, the English government resolved to integrate Ireland into a United Kingdom. Wales had been conquered centuries before by King Edward I; Scotland had been

Plantagenet Descent

amalgamated with England to form Great Britain in 1707; and now Ireland would be integrated into the United Kingdom. To win over the Anglo-Irish Ascendancy who had the most to lose, a handful of English peerages and two dozen new Irish peerages were created, and another two dozen Irish peers obtained a higher rank in the peerage. Four spiritual lords and 28 temporal lords were to sit in the Imperial Parliament in London instead of in the Protestant Irish Parliament in Dublin, and 100 seats in the House of Commons in London were granted to Ireland. The treaty of Union provided:

> . . . the Churches of England and Ireland, as now by law established, be united into one Protestant Episcopal Church, to be called the United Church of England and Ireland; that the doctrine, worship, and government of the said United Church shall be, and shall remain in full force for ever*, as the same are now by law established for the Church of England; and that the continuance and preservation of the said United Church, as the Established Church of England and Ireland, shall be deemed and taken to be an essential and fundamental part of the Union.[147]

The Act of Union was passed by the Parliament in London and received the royal sanction on 1 August 1800. The grand building in which the Irish Parliament had sat was purchased by the Bank of Ireland with secret instructions to alter the chambers to destroy their former appearance as a legislature.

One of those rewarded with an English Peerage was Charles Moore, who had succeeded his father, becoming the 6th Earl of Drogheda, in 1758, and becoming 1st Marquess of Drogheda on 5 July 1791. On 17 January 1801 at the age of 70 he was created Baron Moore of Moore Place in Kent for his support in Parliament

---

* Disestablishment occurred in Ireland in 1870.

of the Act of Union in 1800.[148]

While the list of suffering loyalists compensated William Moore and his in-laws for their financial losses, nothing could ever compensate for the loss of the life of Daniel Moore in the Rebellion of 1798. Walsingham Moore would name two of his sons for his slain brother Daniel: one, a baby, would die in the crossing of the Atlantic in 1817; the other would be born in Canada in 1818.

Little else is known of the life of William Moore between 1800 and 1817 except that by 1817 his wife was dead; his son Walsingham was living in Dublin during at least part of this time (being admitted by seven years service to the Dublin Guild of Barbers and Surgeons some months before the Rebellion of 1798, being married in 1805, and signing himself "of Dublin, gentleman" in 1806); his son Frederick and daughter-in-law Eliza Bolton and his daughter Margaret had emigrated to Canada in 1811, perhaps in part because of the devastating losses suffered by the Boltons in the Rebellion of 1798; and his son William was living in Dublin in 1811 and thereafter.

On Tuesday, 16 May 1817, William Moore, aged about 77 and a widower, left Ireland with his son Walsingham Moore, 49, and family, and his unmarried daughter Anne, on the brig "Mary-Ann," embarking from Wexford for the city of Quebec.

Twelve weeks to the day later, they arrived in Quebec. The "Quebec Mercury" tersely greeted their arrival: "Port of Quebec. Arrived. Aug. 8—Brig Mary-Ann, [Capt.] Barry, 84 days from Wexford, to Geo. Symes, in ballast. Passengers, 126 settlers."[149]

Another branch of the Moore family had arrived in the New World, his son Frederick and daughter-in-law Eliza and his daughter Margaret having settled in Leeds Co., Ontario, when they arrived in Canada in 1811.

Plantagenet Descent

Five weeks after arriving in Canada, William Moore, on 13 September 1817, settled on 100 acres in the County of Leeds, Township of Yonge, near the current town of Athens, Ontario, 250 miles up the St. Lawrence River from the city of Quebec. His son Walsingham Moore on the same day settled on the adjoining 100 acres.[150] Each completed 3 years of residence on his respective holding on 13 September 1820, as noted in an Order in Council dated 25 July 1821. "Walsingham's father came to Canada with him and died three years after arriving in Canada."[151]

On 29 May 1824, William Moore and Walsingham Moore were issued crown grants of their respective 100 acres. William Moore, however, had apparently died between the time of the vesting of his lands and the issuance of the crown grant. William's acreage, having been earned, was eventually put into Walsingham's name.

William is buried next to his son, Frederick, in a private burial ground at the rear of a farmyard under a fieldstone marker bearing the letters WM, which marker was found by Edw. F. Moore and his brother Wm. F. Moore in 1935, at which time the letters were barely visible. The farmyard was then called the Horton Farm and was near New Dublin, Ontario. Frederick's grandson, writing in 1908, stated:

> Frederick Moore, sr., was born in Dublin, Ireland, in the year 1770. While still a young man he took an active part, on the Loyalist side, in the Rebellion of '98. Shortly after this he came to Canada settling on what is now the old Moore Homestead at New Dublin*.
>
> On the farm which he selected for his future home he erected, after the fashion of the times, a log house which was rather large for those early days and which served for many years as a place of worship for the

---

* Were there 300 Moore acres, 100 each owned by Frederick, William, and Walsingham? No effort has been made to trace Frederick's holdings.

members of the Anglican Communion until they were sufficiently strong to erect a church. In this house Frederick Moore spent the remainder of his life and there he eventually died in the year 1848 [on 4 September].

Since William (d. 1820) and Frederick (d. 1848) are buried next to each other, one surmises that Frederick's house continued to be used as a place of worship at least until 1848 and that the private graveyard was adjoining.

William had six children who lived to maturity: Walsingham, Frederick, William, Elizabeth Jane, Anne and Margaret, all but the middle two migrated to Canada.

The Duke of Wellington, 1815
From a painting by Sir T. Lawrence, R.A., at Apsley House.

Chapter 24

Walsingham Moore, gentleman* (1768–1871)
m. 1805
Frances Proctor (1783–1867)

Walsingham Moore was born in Dublin[152] in 1768.[153] His brother Frederick was also born in Dublin, in 1770.[154] Their mother was probably born in Dublin, about 1741. Walsingham Moore's wife-to-be was born in Dublin[155] 3 June 1783. Her father, Walsingham Proctor, was probably born in Dublin, about 1751.

Dublin in 1798 had a population of 200,000, was the second largest city in the British Empire and the seventh largest in the world.

In the Manuscript Room of the Trinity College Library in Dublin in 1993 lie the 200 year old manuscript Minute Books of the "Corporation of Barbers Chirurgeons &c. or Guild of St. Mary Magdalen." They state:

> 13 July [1789] being Quarter Day . . . Walsingham Proctor of Aston's Quay Barber [-Surgeon] admitted to the freedom of the said Guild by Grace Especial (1714–1791, p. 310).
>
> Wednesday the 22nd day of July 1789 . . . Mr. Walsingham Proctor Sworn a ffree Brother (1714–1791, p. 311).
>
> Monday, the 16th of April [1798] being quarter day . . . Mr. Walsingham Moore adm. to the freedom of this

---

* A member of the gentry.

Plantagenet Descent

> Corporation by Service to his ffather* (1792–1822, p. 40).
>
> Saturday, the 23d day of June [1798] . . . Then a ballot took place for Wardens when Walsingham Proctor had 20 votes, Mr. Griffith had 16 votes . . . thereupon Declared Messrs. Proctor and Griffith duly elected, Proctor to be House Warden, Griffith to be the Master Warden (1792–1822, p. 41).

Thus, in 1789 Walsingham Proctor, aged about 38, uncle to Walsingham Moore and for whom Walsingham Moore was named, was admitted "by Grace Especial" to the Dublin "Corporation of Barbers-Surgeons or Guild of St. Mary Magdalen." Membership, beside Guild rights, privileges and duties, also conferred the right to vote for Guild representatives to the City of Dublin Common Council and to vote for members of Parliament. A member was a "Freeman of the City of Dublin," i.e. one enfranchised. Admission to the Guild was limited to barbers, surgeons, apothecaries, and periwig-makers. Admission was by birth (your father apparently had to be a member when you were born), marriage (you married a member's daughter), service (usually seven years)** or grace especial (outstanding citizen).[156]

In 1791 Walsingham Moore, aged 23, had apparently begun the seven-year period of training under the eye of his uncle Walsingham Proctor, although since Walsingham Proctor was admitted

---

* I assume the word "father" is an error for "uncle." Walsingham Proctor would be elected Warden of the 80 man guild at the next meeting. William Moore's name has not been found in the Guild's records. Perhaps on 16 April 1798 William Moore was a barber-surgeon (1) in co. Wexford or (2) retired. The list of "suffering loyalists" would record him as a "yeoman" owning land in co. Wexford two months later.

** The oath of the Barber-Surgeons provided, "You shall not take any Apprentice but of the Protestant religion, and for no less than seven years." Guild Minute Books 1714–1791, Trinity College Library, pp. 52–53.

by "grace especial" as an "outstanding citizen" it is not clear that Walsingham Proctor was a practicing Barber-Surgeon.

Also in 1791, Walsingham Moore's distant cousin, Charles Moore, 6th Earl of Drogheda, was created Marquess of Drogheda. In 1799 Walsingham's other distant cousin, Richard Colley Wellesley, would be created Marquess Wellesley, and in 1812 Arthur Wellesley would be created Marquess (later Duke) of Wellington. In 1802, following the Act of Union, the first edition of Debrett's "Peerage" was published. Walsingham Moore spoke of the fact that he had a relative who was a Marquess.[157] In fact, as noted above, he had three.

As noted, on 16 April 1798, Walsingham Moore, aged 30, was admitted, by service, as a Freeman of the City of Dublin to the Corporation of Barbers-Surgeons or Guild of St. Mary Magdalen.[158]

Two months after Walsingham Moore's admission to the Guild, Faulkner's Journal, Dublin, on 26 June 1798, noted Walsingham Proctor's election, stating, "Saturday last being Election Day in the Corporation of Barbers, Surgeons . . . Mr. Walsingham Proctor [and Mr. Griffith were elected] . . . wardens of said corporation, for the ensuing year."

On 21 June 1801, Walsingham Proctor's daughter, Frances Proctor, born in Dublin and living there, whom Walsingham Moore would marry, was 18 when she wrote in her Book of Common Prayer: "Frances Proctor was born June the 3d in Year of our Lord and god 1783—Susannah Proctor was born on May the 1st in year of our Lord and god 1785. Frances Proctor June 21st 1801 Dublin." One will recall (note 155) that Frances was born in Dublin and that when she was six, in 1789, her father was recognized as a very prominent Dubliner.

Between 1801 and 1805 (ages 18 to 22) Frances Proctor married a man named O'Connor who died shortly thereafter. Her granddaughter, Mrs. Isabella Moore Ross, daughter of Mark Moore,

Plantagenet Descent

told Edw. F. Moore on 14 July 1941: "Her grandfather, Walsingham Moore, married his first cousin, Frances Proctor.[159] Frances was previously married to another man [O'Connor] who lived only a short time after their marriage. Frances Proctor's father and Walsingham's mother were brother and sister. Frances Proctor's family lived in Dublin. Mrs. Ross has the impression that Frances was an only child [had Susannah died early or been forgotten?] and that the family was in reasonably good circumstances."

In 1803, before Walsingham Moore and Frances Proctor married, there occurred in July of that year, in Dublin, the Rebellion of Robert Emmett. This postscript to the Rebellion of 1798 had "myth-making qualities . . . even more pervasive in Irish history than those of 1798 itself."[160] Emmet's plan was to seize Dublin Castle and proclaim the establishment of "the Irish Republic," even though the union of Great Britain and Ireland as the United Kingdom had occurred in 1800. Support for the rebellion came in part from Wexford.[161] The coup failed, and it may have been revulsion against Emmet that led Walsingham Moore to join, in 1803, His Majesty's Corps of Ballaghkeen Yeoman Infantry as a sergeant*, whereas the Rebellion of 1798 itself had not led him to do so.

Walsingham Moore was not the only one to join the yeomanry as a result of Emmet's rebellion. As Lecky was to write: "The short rebellion of Emmet, in 1803 . . . at least furnished the Government with a gratifying proof that the Union [of 1800] had not broken

---

* It is difficult to assess the position of a sergeant in the yeomanry, especially one who was styled a "gentleman" as was Walsingham Moore. Lecky describes only one sergeant: "[the leader of the Wexford rebels was] powerfully supported by Edward Roche . . . a well-to-do farmer of the county [who] had been a sergeant in a yeomanry regiment, and had deserted to the rebels . . . He was soon after elected 'a general officer of the United army of the county of Wexford.'" IV Lecky, p. 446.

the spring of loyalty in Dublin, for the number of yeoman who enlisted there, was even greater than in 1798."[162]

One assumes that Walsingham Moore continued to live in Dublin (with a country residence in co. Wexford) and joined His Majesty's Corps of Ballaghkeen Yeoman Infantry since he had ties to co. Wexford where, in the Rebellion of 1798, his 17-year-old brother, Daniel, a Loyalist, was killed near Gorey, and his 28-year-old brother, Frederick, was "active . . . on the Loyalist side," and where his family and in-laws had property that was damaged, for which the Crown compensated them as "suffering loyalists." The upper classes (gentry and yeomen) formed the yeomanry corps. Most of the populace could not even afford the equipment. It mustered briefly once or twice a year.

In any event, O'Connor "lived only a short time after [his] marriage [to Frances Proctor]" and in 1805 Walsingham Moore and Frances Proctor O'Connor were married, their marriage license being recorded in Ferns, a Diocesan Seat for part of co. Wexford.[163] The marriage was by license (issued by the bishop) rather than by a reading of the banns. Therefore the application was probably made from Frances Proctor O'Connor's country residence and probably Frances and Walsingham did not live in the same parish. Frances was 22, Walsingham was 37.

The next year, in the spring of 1806, Sir Arthur Wellesley, also aged 37, who was one year younger than Walsingham Moore, returned to Dublin after 10 years in India, to marry Kitty Pakenham and to serve as Chief Secretary for Ireland in 1807-1808 at an annual salary of £6,556 before leaving in 1809 to fight the French in the Peninsula Wars.[164] (One of the revolutionary founders of the United Irish Society 15 years earlier had received an annual salary of £50 as a librarian; of such disparities are revolutions made.) An irony of history is that General Sir John Moore, unrelated to the two Moore families under discussion, had, with 3,000

Plantagenet Descent

troops crushed 7,000 rebels in Wexford town in 1798, giving the Anglo- Irish Ascendancy another chance, and, with 29,000 troops against Napoleon's 300,000, fell at Coruña, Spain, in 1809, giving Arthur Wellesley his chance to command the British troops in the Peninsula and become in 1814 the great Duke of Wellington.

Later in 1806, on August 4, in Dublin, "Walsingham Moore of Dublin, gentleman" witnessed a lease of a townhouse in Dublin (in Eastmoreland Park) from George Story to Walsingham Proctor "of South Frederick St. Dublin, gentleman."[165] (In 1993, this street of townhouses is 150 yards long and its north end abuts on Trinity College.) Query whether this property was occupied by Walsingham Moore (and his wife Frances Proctor) as a wedding gift from a benevolent father-in-law and uncle who already had a Dublin residence in South Frederick Street. Or did Walsingham Proctor let the newlyweds live in his South Frederick Street residence while he moved into the Eastmoreland Park residence? Or did the newlyweds live elsewhere in Dublin? The first or third explanation seems the most likely since in 1811 Walsingham Proctor "of Dublin gt." would formally lease the Eastmoreland Park residence to Walsingham Moore's brother William Moore "of sd city, gt."

In 1806, Walsingham Moore and Frances Proctor, living in Eastmoreland Park or elsewhere in Dublin, set about having a family. Their firstborn son was of course named Walsingham Proctor Moore and was born on 27 November 1808. A second son, William Moore, was born on 24 April 1811. Two daughters were born between 1806 and 1810.[166] Perhaps the couple had by 1811 outgrown the Eastmoreland Park property, perhaps they were living elsewhere in Dublin, perhaps they removed full-time to co. Wexford in 1811 to take over properties vacated by Frederick Moore who emigrated to Canada. Perhaps they were annoyed by Walsingham Proctor's remarriage.

In any event, the Eastmoreland Park, Dublin, townhouse was, two months after the birth of Walsingham Moore's second son and fourth child, leased, on 24 June 1811, by Walsingham Proctor "of Dublin, gt." to William Moore "of sd city, gt."[167] This was indeed a benevolent gift by an indulgent uncle to a nephew because Walsingham Proctor was paying an annual rent of £26.3.3d plus taxes for the property and leased it to nephew William for an annual rent of only £16. The deed, a copying out of which is footnoted below, was not recorded for five years. Nephew William Moore at some time accepted the offer from uncle Walsingham Proctor that son-in-law and nephew Walsingham Moore at some time declined: that of a position in the Stamp Office, Dublin. In 1819 William Moore's son would refer to "my father, William Moore, Stamp Office, Dublin." And Inland Revenue in 1951 would certify that "William Moore was employed [in 1829] as a Fourth Stamper in the Stamp Office, Ireland."[168]

1811 was momentous for the Moore family. As noted, Walsingham Moore's brother, Frederick, who was born in 1770, emigrated to Canada. A ms., "A Census for the Township of Elizabethtown for the year 1811," in the Toronto Archives, lists Frederick Moore with 5 males and 2 females in the household. This would include himself, his wife Eliza Bolton (1773-1815), William b. 1794, Sara b. 1798, Richard b. 1800, Walsingham b. 1804, and John B. b. 1808. It would exclude Frederick's sister Margaret, who traveled to Canada with him and apparently married soon after arrival, and include a son born in Canada. Frederick Moore's name does not appear in the 1808 or 1810 census.

It was perhaps in 1811 that Walsingham Proctor remarried to the great displeasure of his daughter Frances.

So 1811 may have been the year of three significant events: First, Frederick emigrated to Canada. Second, Walsingham Proctor's second marriage may have occurred. Third, Walsingham

Moore may have vacated the Eastmoreland Park, Dublin, townhouse, either to move elsewhere in Dublin or to Wexford.

1815 brought a third son and fifth child to Walsingham Moore and Frances Proctor. Four months after the Battle of Waterloo, Frederick Moore was born on 28 October 1815. The baby was obviously named for Walsingham Moore's brother who was now into his fourth year in Canada.

1817 brought two developments: (1) Walsingham Moore's decision, implemented on 16 May 1817, to join his brother Frederick in Canada, and (2) the birth of Walsingham's fourth son and sixth child, Daniel, named for Walsingham's brother who had been killed in the Rebellion of 1798. We do not know the names of Walsingham Moore's two daughters; we do know they were born between 1806 and 1810.

Frederick Moore's emigration to Canada in 1811 had been very unusual. Walsingham's emigration in 1817 was much less so. The exodus from Britain and Ireland was essentially a post-Napoleonic Wars phenomenon. It began when the first peace came in 1814: 7,000 left Ireland for Newfoundland. It increased in 1815 even though the events leading up to Waterloo had delayed it until late summer, when the normal season for transatlantic travel was over. The flood began in 1816, particularly toward the end of it since 1816 was "the year without a summer" in Europe. There was torrential rain and sleet and snow during the entire summer, destroying harvests and causing distress and starvation in both town and country. Meanwhile, the customary postwar industrial recession was ravaging the cities. In 1817 20,000 immigrants came from the United Kingdom to the U. S., although the U. K. authorities tried to steer all of their emigrants to Canada, which probably received more than 20,000 during that year. These were almost entirely Protestants who were relatively well fixed and could afford the fare.[169] They came, in general, because of overpopulation at home, fear of famine, free land, low taxes and a burning desire for greater freedom. The third great diastole or expansion of the Protestant Ascendancy that had begun in the 1640s had ended. The third great systole or contraction had begun, but the Moores would not be there to witness or participate in it.

Walsingham's decision was taken before the bad news for 1817 was in: "In 1817 came the first serious Irish famine of the century . . . a particularly terrible famine with thousands of deaths."[170]

An irony but commonplace of fate is that the glorious victory by Walsingham Moore's distant cousin, the Duke of Wellington, at Waterloo in 1815 resulted in the end of the Napoleonic Empire and the demobilization of the British army and the armaments industry, which led directly to the recession in the United Kingdom in 1816. This recession in turn led to the "large-sale emigration to Canada and the U.S."[171] So, as much as any factor, the Duke's victory caused his cousin's departure from Ireland.

On 5 May 1817, H. G. Bourney, Lieutenant, certified, "These are to certify that Walsingham Moore of Cullintra *[sic]* in the parish of Monamolin and county of Wexford in Ireland aforesaid, having served in [His Majesty's Corps of Ballaghkeen Yeoman Infantry] fourteen years as a sergant *[sic]*—during which he conducted himself to the entire satisfaction of his officers and is in consequence of his intention of leaving this country—Discharged."

Walsingham Moore embarked from Wexford, eleven days after his discharge, on the brig "Mary-Ann," on Tuesday, 16 May 1817, with his wife, 2 daughters, 4 sons (the baby Daniel died during the crossing), his father and an unmarried sister, Anne, who was considered part of father William's household.

The details of Walsingham Moore's arrival in Quebec city and settlement five weeks later, on 100 acres, near the present town of Athens, Ontario, are given in the preceding chapter.[172] On their arrival, his acres and his father's acres were heavily forested except for a cleared quarter-acre with an abandoned squatters shanty.

The family continued to grow. Three sons were born to Walsingham Moore in Canada: Daniel Moore, born 18 August 1818, and named for the baby who had died during the Atlantic crossing, Mark Moore, born 30 November 1820, and Edward Cooke Howard Moore, born on 25 January 1822. The name "Cooke" was apparently in honor of Frances Cooke Proctor, grandmother of both parents, and her father, Walsingham Cooke. Maybe there was even a memory of the Sir Walsingham Cooke who in 1640 owned 3,131 acres in co. Wexford, including some in Cullentra in the parish of Monamolin where Walsingham had lived when mustering out of the corps in 1817.

We don't know if Walsingham Moore was a surgeon, an apothecary, a barber or a periwig-maker, either in Athens or Dublin or Wexford, although there probably wasn't much call on the last of these arts in Athens.

Walsingham Moore was apparently content. He had with him his wife, 6 sons, and 2 daughters. His brother Frederick lived nearby, as did his two now-married sisters, Anne and Margaret. Anne had come over with Walsingham in 1817 and Margaret with Frederick in 1811. His usual comment to his son Mark when the latter returned from town was, "What's fresh, Mark?" Walsingham Moore himself remained fresh, living to the age of 103. He was 52 when Mark was born, 54 when Edward Cooke Howard was born, and 75 when Mark married.

So, Walsingham Moore, "gentleman of the city of Dublin," was now a farmer near the town of Athens, Ontario. Thomas Jefferson the gentleman farmer of Monticello would live to 1826 but Walsingham Moore, who was born before the American Revolution began, would live until the American Civil War was over, and

father, Louis Rosenwater, had been born on 11 May 1850 in Aparias, Austria-Hungary (now Presov, Slovakia), an early stronghold of the Reformation, which reflects itself in the fact that Louis Rosenwater was a Presbyterian who joined the Masons on his 21st birthday in 1871. Aparias had been founded as a German colony in the 12th century and was one of the 24 settlements along the trade route from east Hungary to Poland. The family regarded itself as German Protestants. Blanche's mother, Sarah Black, had been born on 5 March 1855, also in Aparias, Austria-Hungary.[183]

"Louis Rosenwater was born May 11, 1850, at Aparias, Austria-Hungary, and five years later, Sarah Black (who was to become his wife) was born in the same house, in the very same bed, her family having moved to the house vacated by the Rosenwaters. The two families were close friends, and it was only natural that when Mr. Rosenwater came to this country when he was 15 years old [in 1865], and settled in Cairo [Illinois] where his older brother, Sam, was in business, that he should [soon] make his home with the Black family, who had previously come to America [to Cleveland in 1856] when their daughter [Sarah] was only a year old. He lived in the Black home where Mrs. Black was a mother to Mr. Rosenwater.

"On October 12, 1879 Mr. and Mrs. Rosenwater were married [he being 29, she being 24], and thus a childhood romance was continued for more than half a century; the fiftieth [wedding] anniversary being celebrated four years ago [in 1929]."[184]

Louis Rosenwater was the son of Aaron Rosenwater (a farmer and hotel keeper), who was born in 1798 a "native of Germany" and died in Europe in 1872, and of Leah Gross, also a "native of Germany," who was born in 1809. Louis's brother, Samuel, born in 1840, emigrated to Cleveland in 1860, where the Blacks had been living since 1856; Samuel, in 1863, moved to Cairo, Illinois,

Plantagenet Descent

at the juncture of the Ohio and Mississippi Rivers. Louis, in 1865, emigrated from Presov to join his brother in Cairo. In 1883 their mother was living in Cairo with Samuel and his family. Samuel and Louis were ardent members of the Republican Party.

Sarah Black was the daughter of Adolf Black and Ressie Neiman, both born in 1823, who married in 1844 and emigrated with their children to Cleveland in 1856. Adolf was the son of Leopold (a landlord) and Betty Black. In 1867 the Blacks followed Samuel Rosenwater from Ohio to Cairo. The following year Fannie Black, born in 1850, married Samuel, and 11 years later Sarah Black married Louis. Their daughter, Blanche, was born 10 months later, on 18 August 1880. Adolf manufactured shoes and boots and had a retail outlet in Cairo, and had a son who was a lawyer and legislator. Samuel and a partner owned a dry goods and clothing store in Cairo. Before 1883 Louis and Sarah and their daughter Blanche moved from Cairo, Illinois, to Sikeston, Missouri, 25 miles away*. In 1889 they moved another 25 miles to Dexter, Missouri, and in 1900 to Kennett, Missouri. They owned restaurants and bakeries.

The wedding of Ralph Henry Moore, 33, and Blanche Eloise Rosenwater, 26, took place in Kennett, Missouri, on Wednesday, 22 May 1907. The ceremony was performed by the Rev. Nelson B. Henry, D.D., pastor of the Methodist Episcopal Church, South. The unidentified Kennett newspaper account of the wedding stated in part:

> A more delightful occasion could not be imagined. The principals are popular young people here, the bride being noted for her sweet disposition, excellent traits and devotion to home and friends.
>
> Mr. Moore came here from Minnesota, a year ago, as

---

* William Henry Perrin, ed., History of Alexander, Union and Pulaski Counties, Illinois (1883), Part V, pp. 7, 40–41.

Ralph Henry Moore, Sr.

manager of an extensive timber business, and during his residence here has impressed all as being a business man of steady purpose and in every way a worthy citizen.

The bride was becomingly attired in a white Paris muslin, over white taffeta, made in Princess effect, trimmed in Valenciennes lace; it was round length; high corsage. She carried a bouquet of roses and maiden-hair ferns. Her coiffure was high.

The bridesmaid, Miss Ione Rosenwater, was gowned in pink crepe de chine. She carried a bouquet of pink carnations. Dr. W. F. Gerhardt [who later married the bridesmaid and thereby became brother-in-law of the bride] was the best man.

It was a noticed fact that the gowns worn on this occasion were the most elegant of any in the history of Kennett.

The happy couple will remain here for the present, but will, in warmer weather, take an extended trip through the lakes and Canada, where Mr. Moore spent his boyhood days.

He was 5 feet 8 inches with brown hair and gray eyes. She was 5 feet 6 inches with brown hair and gray eyes. The couple had three children: Rose Virginia Moore (b. 14 March 1908 in Kennett, m. Eduard Lord, a publisher in Hawaii, had two children, and d. in Hawaii); Ralph Henry (Jack) Moore, Jr. (b. 26 July 1909 in Kennett, m. Estelle Hero, d. in Duluth 12 April 1980); and Fanny Ione Moore (b. 13 June 1915 in Kennett, d. 9 April 1956).

On 13 October 1913, aged 39 and a resident of Kennett, Ralph Henry Moore, Sr., a citizen of Great Britain and Ireland, became a citizen of the United States. In 1917, Ralph (aged 44) and Blanche removed to Duluth, Minnesota*. Ralph continued in the timber business with Duluth as his base and Curry & Whyte as

---

* Blanche's brother joined the army.

his company (1920 city directory) until his retirement in 1936 at the age of 63*. Ralph died on 16 January 1945, aged 71, in Duluth, of lateral sclerosis, after a long illness. His wife died on 8 January 1964, aged 83, in a nursing home in Walker, Minn., of pneumonia and old age. Both were communicants of St. Paul's Episcopal Church, Duluth. They are buried at Park Hill Cemetery in Duluth.

✧ ✧ ✧

Duluth was a magnet for many. Five years after the early death in 1881 of Ralph's mother in Brockville, her brother Alfred Gillon, 32, was a Municipal Court Officer in Duluth, a steamship voyage of a thousand miles up the Great Lakes from Brockville. The 1886 Duluth Directory states, "No city on the continent has shown . . . so great an increase in the last six years." The population continued to explode as people streamed from Canada, the Midwest and Europe to the burgeoning city that shipped the western grain and the northern iron-ore and lumber that the network of railroads poured into Duluth, making it the second largest port in the country. The population soared from 3,470 in 1880 to a then-estimated 60,000 at the end of the decade.

In 1886 the membership of Duluth's St. Paul's Episcopal Church, of which Ralph would become a parishioner, was 146. The membership of the Polish Catholic Church (about which more later) was 2,000. In 1888 Alfred Gillon was joined in Duluth by his brothers Henry K., 28, a "wood foreman," and James F., 26, a butcher in the shop owned by Duluth's Mayor. In 1889 the three Gillon brothers were reunited in Duluth with their 70-

---

* Three years earlier, on 14 November 1933, Blanche's father died at the age of 83 in Kennett, Missouri of "decompensated heart." The elaborate funeral services were "conducted by the Rev. J. E. Travis, pastor of the Presbyterian Church, assisted by the Rev. Daniel Morgan and the Rev. F. M. Love." 1933 unidentified Kennett newspaper obit. Blanche's mother, Sarah Black, died on 28 September 1948, aged 93 years, 7 months, in Kennett of "congestive heart failure."

year-old mother (Ralph's grandmother) "Ann Gillon (widow of Henry)." In 1891 Robert J. Gillon, 41, the fourth and last and oldest of Ralph's Gillon uncles came to Duluth. The 1892 Directory predicted, "Duluth's destiny is to become *the great* city of the interior of this continent." That year Miss [Lillian] Letitia Gillon, Ralph's aunt, became the proprietress of Duluth's South Side Meat Market. James became the manager. Ralph's older brother, Mark Alfred Moore, about to be 20, left Ontario for Duluth and in December Ralph, 19, and his younger brother Charles P., 17, followed. Mark married and had a son, Charles C., born in 1893, who would be living in San Francisco in 1908, aged 15.

In 1896 Ralph was living in Duluth with Grandma Ann Gillon as were James and Anna, his wife. Ralph, 23, was the proprietor of a meat market, explaining his son's later expertise at selecting and cooking great cuts. Mark would be dead within the year from TB at the age of 25. Alf and Robert Gillon would each become second in command of the Duluth Police Department; Henry K. would become Sheriff and then Chief of Police of Two Harbors, Minn. Stanislaw Konczak and his wife and 3-year-old daughter Josephine (see next chapter) arrived in Duluth from Chicago and settled three blocks west of Ann Gillon, whose great grandson Ralph Henry Moore, Jr. would, 34 years later, marry Stanislaw's granddaughter Estelle Hero, whose father Walter Haro would come to Duluth from Poland in 1898. By 1900 Ralph was in the timber business and travelling the country*.

---

* Ralph's grandmother Ann Gillon who was born in Ireland on 14 June 1819 died in Duluth on 19 December 1908 when Ralph, just married, was living in Kennett, Mo. Ann is buried in Forest Hill Cemetery in Duluth. She had 9 children: Jane Speedie b. 1844; Fanny Moore b. 1848; Robert J. b. 1850–d. Salem Ore. 1938; Lillian L. b.1852; Alfred b. 1854–d. Duluth 1916; Angeline Hamilton b. 1856; Carrie McNairnay b. 1858; Henry K. b. 1860–retired to Salem Ore. in 1931; and James F. b. 1862–living in Addie, Idaho in 1908.

Ralph Henry Moore, Jr. and Estelle Marguerite Hero, 1930.

Chapter 28

Ralph Henry (Jack) Moore, Jr. (1909–1980)
m. 1930
Estelle Marguerite Hero (1911–1968)

Ralph Henry (Jack) Moore, Jr., was born in Kennett, Missouri, on 26 July 1909, the only son and second child of Ralph Henry Moore, Sr., and Blanche Eloise Rosenwater. Like his father, Jack was a middle child. Jack's father had moved from his parents' home to his aunt's home in 1881 when he was seven and his mother died. Jack's mother had moved from Cairo, Illinois, to Missouri before 1883 when she was three and her parents moved. Jack moved from Kennett, Missouri, to Duluth, Minnesota, in 1917 when he was eight and his parents moved.

On 15 September 1930, during the depths of the Great Depression, Jack eloped at the age of 21 to Eveleth, Minnesota, with Estelle Marguerite Hero, age 19. He was strikingly handsome, 5 feet 11 inches in height with jet black hair (which had been white as a child), a cleft chin and bright blue eyes, strongly resembling the movie actor Tyrone Power. She was strikingly beautiful, 5 feet 2 inches in height with brown hair and hazel eyes, strongly resembling the movie actress Marlene Dietrich.

Estelle was born in Duluth, Minnesota, on 12 April 1911, the eldest of five children of Walter Hero (son of Stanislaw Chara*)

---

* Walter named his firstborn "Estelle" (Stanislawa) in honor of his father. The surname "Chara" (dear beloved) derives, according to a

and Josephine Konczak (daughter of Stanislaw [Stanley] Konczak and Jadwiga [Ida] Wlasna). Walter was born in Lublin, Poland, long occupied and industrialized by Russia, on 24 March 1886. At the age of 12 he left his parents and 3-year-old brother Joseph in Poland to come to the U.S. alone and on to Duluth doubtless to live with a now unknown friend or relative who may have met him on arrival. Four years earlier, Walter's one-year-old wife-to-be had come with her family to Chicago from German-occupied Poland. After two years in Chicago, her family came to Duluth, two years ahead of him. Before coming, both her family and Walter doubtless knew other Poles in Duluth, a then burgeoning city. During the decade preceding 1890, Duluth had had a sensational 10-fold growth in population, to 33,115, with the development of the railways, of commerce on Lake Superior, and of the iron mines of northern Minnesota*. By 1928 Duluth had quadrupled in size, to 116,920. In 1928, Walter, aged 42, visited Poland. We have a photograph taken then of him, his parents, his two brothers, Joseph and Michael, his two sisters, and four of their children, one of whom, Stanley Chara (son of Joseph), was born in 1922, survived both Russian and Nazi prisoner-of-war camps as a member of the Polish and British Air Forces, came to Chicago in 1954 and is living in Schiller Park, Illinois, in 1994. Walter was a manager at the Globe Iron Works in Duluth, owned rental properties, was a member of the Eagles, Oswiata, Centralla and the Polish National Alliance, of which he was secretary. He died on 26 January 1943, aged 56, of coronary thrombosis following an assault by a fellow Alliance member after a heated political de-

---

 family tradition, from an ancestor in the retinue of the beautiful Bona Sforza, daughter of the Duke of Milan, who came from Italy to Poland to become Queen in 1518.

* As noted in the previous chapter, Ralph Henry Moore, 19, joined his mother's then-settled family (the Gillons) in Duluth in 1892.

bate. He was a member of the Polish National Catholic Church. His wife, Josephine, was born in Odolanow, Province of Poznan, Poland, occupied by Germany for a century, on 25 February 1893, came to Chicago with her parents, three siblings and maternal grandmother at the age of one and to Duluth at the age of three. She was a member of St. Josephat's National Catholic Church and Queen Wanda Lodge of the Polish National Alliance. She died on 1 August 1966, aged 73, of cancer of the pancreas. Walter and Josephine had married in Duluth on 22 May 1910 when he was 24 and she was 17. After Walter's death she married his best friend Tom Bardak, who was born in Poland, came to Duluth in 1902, aged 18, and died 6 January 1963. Josephine survived him. Both Walter and Josephine are buried with her parents and maternal grandmother in the Polish Cemetery in Duluth*.

---

* Josephine's father, Stanley Konczak, born 15 April 1854 in Poland died 25 September 1930 in Duluth, aged 76, of uremia; Josephine's mother, Ida Wlasna, born 15 October 1863 in Poland died 4 October 1928 in Duluth, aged 65, of diabetes mellitus. Ida's mother, Magdalina, born 20 April 1827 in Poland died 25 April 1923 in Duluth, aged 96, of acute gastritis. Magdalina was the daughter of Kzizan Garbarczyk ("son of the tanner," an echo of William the Conqueror, whose maternal grandfather was a tanner). Magdelina married, before 1858, Christopher Wlasny (pronounced Vwasny). They had 5 daughters, all born in or close to Raszkow, near Odolanow—equidistant from Berlin and Warsaw—in germanized Posen (Poznan) Province. Before 1888 Magdalina's son-in-law John Dembik and wife Josephine left for Bernburg, Germany, SW of Berlin. In 1892 son-in-law Paul Cegla and wife Rose emigrated to Denham, Minn. In 1894 son-in-law Stanley Konczak, and wife Ida, 4 children and Magdalina left Posen Province for Chicago and then Duluth. Ida's 3 remaining sisters with their families eventually left Europe to join the Konczaks in Duluth: Josephine Dembik (1866–1944) in 1901, Veronica Uzarek (1868–1934) in 1910, Victoria Sojka (1858–1951) in 1914. In the quarter century ending in 1914, 4 million Poles, perhaps 20% of the population, emigrated, primarily to the U.S.

Jack and Estelle had two children, Thomas R(onald) Moore, born 27 March 1932, and Marilyn Estelle Moore, born 27 June 1933, married 1st Stanley Watts, married 2d Lawrence Shenette, died 11 October 1987, aged 54, of lung and esophageal cancer, being a heavy smoker. She was survived by her three children: Thomas Watts Shenette, Toni Lynn Shenette Olsen, Tracy Shenette.

Jack had followed his father into the timber business, but during the Great Depression he entered government service, ran for public office, served as Chief of Detectives, reentered the business world as an entrepreneur who owned a number of businesses.

Jack played semi-pro hockey as a sport as a young man and was an active outdoorsman all of his life. One stirring episode occurred on 12 February 1939, when he was playing goalie in the Duluth Amphitheatre before thousands of spectators and the building began to collapse. He ran en pointe into the stands, swept his two children, then aged five and six, one under each arm, and ran from the crashing structure to safety. Still on skates he then directed rescue operations.

In 1945, at the age of 36, he volunteered and served in the U. S. Army. Shades of his great-great-grandfather, Walsingham Moore, who, in 1803 at the age of 35, had enlisted in His Majesty's Corps of Ballaghkeen Yeoman Infantry.

On 27 March 1968, on their son's 36th birthday, Estelle died suddenly, aged 56 (the age at which her father died), at home in Duluth, three years after open heart surgery at the Mayo Clinic, from failure of the artificial valve. As a child she had had rheumatic fever which had impaired her heart. On 12 April 1980, Jack, aged 70, died on his wife's birthday, of lung and intestinal cancer, being a heavy smoker. Estelle and then Jack were buried with her parents, maternal grandparents and great grandmother in the Polish Cemetery in Duluth.

Thomas R. Moore

Margaret Clarissa King

The Armorial Ensigns of
THOMAS RONALD MOORE Esq.
Moorish Castle, Point O'Woods, NY, C St.J, BA Yale, JD Harvard, Bar of NY and US Supreme Court

College of Arms
London

Lancaster Herald

Willard Sean Moore

Margaret Else Nelson

Elizabeth Margaret Clarissa Moore

Charles Ralph Henry Moore

Sarah Elizabeth Moore and her parents
1994

Chapter 29

Thomas R(onald) Moore, Esq.[*] (1932–)
m. 1955
Margaret Clarissa King (1932–)

Thomas R. Moore was born in Duluth, Minnesota, on 27 March 1932, the firstborn of Ralph Henry Moore, Jr., and Estelle Marguerite Hero. His only sibling, Marilyn Estelle Moore, was born 15 months later on 27 June 1933.

When he was four, he saved his sister's life when she fell into a creek and he drew her out with a fallen branch.

When he was five, his father bought a new house (further from the creek). The sellers kept postponing the closing, apparently not to the distress of his father, who did not insist that time was of the essence. But this legal position was not communicated to Tom, who walked to the new residence, asked for the owner, Mr. Fisher, and announced, "Mr. Fisher, if you don't move out tomorrow, I'm going to kick this house down."

In grade school he was Captain of the Write-a-Fighter Corps, which wrote letters to servicemen in World War II, who included his four uncles, an aunt and his father, and was Captain of his school's and Chief of his city's schoolboy police.

---

[*] Since the 14th century the higher echelons of lawyers and since 1620 all lawyers have been entitled to the rank of "Esquire." Sir Anthony Wagner, English Genealogy, p. 117.

Arms of William King. Settled in Salem, Mass. 1636. Crosier, *General Armory, A Register of American Families Entitled to Coat Armor* (1957), p. 81.

Thomas R(onald) Moore, Esq.

When he was fourteen, in the epidemic of September 1946, he was stricken with polio, like President Roosevelt; he was told he would never walk again, but recovered to walk with only a slight limp.

When he was eighteen, he graduated from Duluth Central High School with a straight "A" average and as President of the Student Council.

He matriculated at Yale University in 1950 where he was an officer of the Varsity Debate Team, an officer of the Yale Political Union, one of eleven Scholars of the House in a class of 1,000, Class Marshall, and was graduated B.A. *magna cum laude* in 1954.

He declined Yale's offer to be Clare Scholar at Cambridge University (similar to the Rhodes Scholars but more exclusive) and Yale Law School's offer of a place, to accept Harvard Law School where he matriculated in 1954. There he won the Roscoe Pound Prize for Moot Court and scored the highest mark in his class in taxation, which prompted an accepted offer to teach at the Harvard Law School International Program in Taxation during his third year at law school.

During his first year at Harvard Law School, Steve Kumble, a Yale and Harvard Law School classmate whom Tom had unsuccessfully coached to become a Varsity debater, introduced Tom to the Wall Street law firm of Donovan Leisure with such glowing reviews that Donovan Leisure hired Tom for the summer of 1955 as the first first-year law student ever hired for the summer by a major Wall Street law firm.

Later during that summer of 1955, Tom married, on 10 September 1955, in Chicago, Margaret Clarissa King, only child of the prominent Chicago lawyer and author Willard Leroy King (National Cyclopedia of American Biography) and Margaret Amelia Erickson. Willard King was a descendant in the tenth generation of William King*, who settled in Salem, Mass. in 1636, and of the

Mayflower Pilgrim Stephen Hopkins**, of Capt. Simon Willard*** who founded Concord, Mass. in 1635[185], of Thomas Yale, grand-

---

* William King sailed from Weymouth, England to Salem, Mass. on 20 March 1635/6 on the *Abigail*, which bore 106 passengers, including William, a Puritan aged 40, his wife, Dorithie Hayne, aged 34, and five children, Mary, 12; Katherine, 10; William, 8; Hannah, 6; and Samuel, 2. William was made a freeman (voter) on 25 May 1636 and given two 40 acre grants, on the second of which, in Ryalside (now Beverly), he built his homestead. William was armigerous. W. A. Crosier, *General Armory, A Register of American Families Entitled to Coat Armor* (1957), p. 81, lists him, "KING. Massachusetts. William King, Salem, 1595–1651. (Uxborough, Devon.) Sable, on a chevron between three crosses-crosslet or [gold], as many escallops as of the field. CREST -An escallop [pilgrim's badge] or. KING. Long Island. Samuel King, Southold, 1633–1721. Same Arms as William King, Salem, Mass." (Illustration shown.) On William's death in January 1650/1, his second son, Samuel, aged 17, left Salem with his mother and several sisters to settle in Southold, Long Island, New York. Samuel died on 29 November 1721, aged 88. Mary, one of his seven children, married Lord Gardiner on 24 June 1687. Their eldest son became 4th Lord of the Manor in 1738. Samuel was Willard King's ancestor.

** Stephen Hopkins may be the only person to have lived in America before sailing on the *Mayflower* (from Plymouth, England, to Plymouth, Mass.) on 16 September 1620 (N.S.) to found New England. On 2 June 1609 he had sailed from London on the *Sea Venture* to Jamestown, Va., but the ship was severely damaged in a hurricane, casting the company ashore in Bermuda, giving rise to Shakespeare's *The Tempest*. After a sojourn in Jamestown, he returned to London, and in 1620 was one of the Londoners recruited for the *Mayflower* voyage. One of three of 102 *Mayflower* passengers called "Master," he was one of 17 freemen (voters). He sailed with two male servants, his second wife, and three children. His second son, Oceanus, was born aboard the *Mayflower*. He built and owned the first wharf in Plymouth Colony and was referred to as "merchant," "planter," "Gentleman," and "Master." Born in 1581, he died in Plymouth in 1644, having had nine children, leaving a fair estate of £130. John D. Austin, *Mayflower Families through Five Generations*, vol. 6, pp. 3–7 (1992).

Thomas R(onald) Moore, Esq.

father of Elihu Yale, and of the 18th century scientific writer George Cadogan Morgan[186]. Margaret Erickson's ancestors may have landed but did not settle in New England c. 1000, preferring Iceland.

Tom is 6 feet 1 inch tall with blond hair and blue eyes. Margaret is 5 feet 6 inches with brown hair and brown eyes. Margaret was born on 10 July 1932, in Chicago, was graduated from the University of Chicago Laboratory School, Lake Forest Academy, and Connecticut College for Women where she was first in her class, was elected to Phi Beta Kappa in her junior year, and was editor of the literary magazine. She was one of ten college graduates selected for the *Time-Life* Training Program in 1954 and from 1955 to 1957 was a model, Assistant Fashion and Features Editor and a bylined writer for the *Boston Herald-Traveller*. Tom and Margaret have three children: Willard Sean b. 1 April 1958, Elizabeth Margaret Clarissa b. 4 February 1960, and Charles Ralph Henry b. 22 April 1963. After the youngest child went off to prep school, Margaret became Director of Development for The Spence School; then Associate Director of Public Affairs—and in 1993 Director of Special Events—for The New York Hospital-Cornell Medical Center. As the only child of Willard King, she is armigerous, her arms being those of William King, described above. Illustration shown.

Upon graduation from Harvard Law School in 1957 with a J.D., Tom accepted an offer to become an associate at the prestigious Manhattan law firm of Dewey Ballantine. Gov. Thomas E. Dewey

---

***Simon Willard was also armigerous. Crosier, supra, p. 137, lists him, "WILLARD. Massachusetts. Capt. Simon Willard, Cambridge, 1634 [Kent.] Argent, a chevron ermines [black with white spots] between three flasks ppr. CREST -A griffin's head erased [jagged neck] or [gold]." The family was "originally VILLIARD of Caen in Normandy, seated in co. Sussex temp. Edward III." Burke, *General Armory* (1969), entry Willard.

had just joined the firm of several hundred lawyers after twice losing the Presidential election, first to Franklin Delano Roosevelt and then to Harry S Truman, before engineering the election of Dwight David Eisenhower. Wall Street law firms in those benighted days offered more prestige than money (although more money than other law firms). The top salary was $5,500 a year. Associates on the partnership track were expected to work most days from 9:30 a.m. to midnight, so the salary averaged out to less than $2 an hour.

Typical of Tom's work at Dewey Ballantine was his victory for the charitable foundation named as beneficiary under the mutilated will of Oscar B. Cintas. To put several years' work into three sentences: Tom devised the irrefutable argument that if the opponents of Cintas's will were to prevail, they would net nothing since the decline in value of the stocks in the estate immediately following Cintas's death was so great that the Federal estate tax would exceed the present value of the estate. Accordingly, a compromise should be worked out whereby the foundation would receive all the assets (thus creating a full charitable deduction for the estate based on date-of-death values) and pay a relatively small dollar settlement to the contestants. Thus he preserved Cintas's collection of Old Masters for the foundation*.

Two years before his class of 1957 was up for partnership consideration at Dewey Ballantine, Tom received two unsolicited partnership offers: One was from Windels Marx Davies & Ives. At that time Charles Agamain was the comptroller of the Chase Manhattan Bank (a Dewey Ballantine client) and he recommended Tom to Paul Windels who was looking for a tax partner; Agamain had developed a procedure of calling Tom the day before board meetings and posing legal questions that might arise at the

---

* As an illustration of the continuity of life, he has been engaged in 1993 as an expert witness in a London trial involving some of those paintings.

Thomas R(onald) Moore, Esq.

meeting so that he could say, "I'm not a lawyer but it seems to me that . . . " The second partnership offer was from Breed Abbott & Morgan. Tom accepted it, being impatient with a projected two-year wait at Dewey Ballantine.

At Breed Abbott, Tom developed a clientele of his own that brought in over a million dollars a year in legal fees, and he also serviced the firm's other clients. Among the clients he attracted (by besting their lawyer in negotiations in their first encounter) were James Sinclair and Vincent Tese, whose brokerage firm made many fortunes by accumulating gold, leveraged 20 to 1, as gold rose from 80 to 800, before shorting it at the same leverage all the way down to 350. In connection with financing a strategic metals fund, Bob Foman, the Chairman of E. F. Hutton, asked Tom to suggest world-class figures of unimpeachable integrity for the Board, and Tom responded with two friends, his distant cousin Valerian Wellesley the 8th Duke of Wellington and General Lucius Clay, Jr. Tom also represented Sinclair, Tese and George Ring in the development and later sale to TCI of their cable TV companies. Tom won a $14 million n.o.l. litigation for Sippican Corporation, worked on J. Walter Thompson issues and Avon Products matters. He so impressed Wayne Hicklin, the Chairman of Avon, that Wayne named Tom Executor of his will, saying that he was the "smartest guy" he had ever met. Such brilliance bred hostility and envy in some of his partners.

When Breed Abbott refused to modernize its ways, Tom, in 1984, after 19 years at Breed Abbott, resigned his partnership to become a partner and tax department head at Finley, Kumble, Wagner, Heine, Underberg, Manley & Casey, one of the three largest law firms in the nation with 800 lawyers and thousands of employees. It was founded and run by Tom's Yale and Harvard Law classmate, Steve Kumble.

At Finley Kumble, Tom continued to attract clients: the firm's receipts from his clients rose toward $2 million a year. He did a billion dollars of municipal bond financing and won major tax court victories. He worked long hours and enjoyed himself. But the internecine bloodletting among the name partners at Finley Kumble tore the firm apart. The major players left and the firm collapsed. Tom became a partner in the bond firm of Hawkins Delafield & Wood to do bond work and create a tax department and a corporate department for Hawkins, but the firm was paralyzed. After two years Tom left in 1990 to start his own firm with the idea he could charge clients less and keep more without the overhead he had lived with for so many years. His income skyrocketed.

Tom had reached the height of his profession. He was included in *Who's Who in the World*, *Who's Who in America* and the *Social Register*. The *American Lawyer* referred to him as "the renowned international tax lawyer." The *Legal Times* called him "the establishment lawyer." He wrote law review articles and gave pop legal commentaries on TV. He was also active in volunteer efforts. For example, years earlier he had accepted the presidency of the National Society to Prevent Blindness (a national health agency) after thrice intelligently refusing that crown of thorns. He knowingly accepted the presidency when the Society was within weeks of bankruptcy, which he averted. After years of non-paid effort on his part, the Society had an annual income and a net worth both in the eight figures. He was rewarded, indirectly, by being inducted by Queen Elizabeth II, his ninth cousin once removed, into The Most Venerable Order of The Hospital of St. John of Jerusalem, founded in 1113, where he became a Commander. He did similar things for other societies, such as Confrérie de la Chaîne des Rôtisseurs, an international wine and food society, chartered in 1248 by Saint Louis, King of France, composed of connoisseurs and professional chefs, which, as National President, he, with a handful of aides, raised to national consciousness.

From a financial standpoint, more important than his earnings

Thomas R(onald) Moore, Esq.

as a lawyer, Tom had (on the advice of his distant cousin Edw. F. Moore) become a limited partner of Michael Steinhardt in Steinhardt Partners. He also became a limited partner in several other hedge funds. These hedge funds returned 25% to 50% annually, year after year.

With those returns Tom was able to finance his family with homes in Manhattan, Connecticut, Long Island and Colorado, and Willard (Exeter, Yale, Berkeley Law) in a real-estate business (Mayflower Associates in NYC) in addition to his law practice, Clarissa (Andover, Yale, Dartmouth MBA) in a money management business (Calport Asset Management, Inc.) with partners Art Laffer (of the Laffer Curve) and Michael Petrino, and Charles (Taft, Tulane) as the owner-chef of Evangeline's the renowned white tablecloth restaurant in the cool ski-resort of Telluride, Colorado.

The Queen, through the College of Arms in London, granted inheritable arms to Tom. They are azure (Yale blue background) in pale (ancestor Sir Richard Cooke was Principal Secretary of State and Chancellor of the Exchequer in the Irish Pale) gules (Harvard Law crimson) flanked argent (sandy slopes of Moorish Castle) on pale three annulets gold (1. for ancestors who were Kings of England for three centuries, 2. for Margaret King, mother of his three children and 3. for Sir Richard who borne three red annulets on his arms) between two sets of three demi lions passant gold issuing from flanks and pale (royal arms). Crest: Moor cock (Moore, progenitor) gules holding Maltese Cross argent fitchy (Commander, Order of St. John). Motto: SINE MORE NIHIL (without law nothing, without Moore nothing, without more nothing).

Tom is a member of the Order of the Crown of Charlemagne because of his direct descent in the 40th generation from the Emperor Charlemagne, and of the Magna Charta Barons because

Plantagenet Descent

of his direct descent in the 26th generation from Henry de Bohun, 1st Earl of Hereford, one of the 25 barons who were guarantors of Magna Carta in 1215, and of The Plantagenet Society because of his direct descent from four Plantagenet Kings.

Plantagenet Descent

Thomas R. Moore's direct ancestor, William the Conqueror, had Baldwin, his cousin, as one of his Companions at the Battle of Hastings in 1066. After victory, William conferred upon Baldwin much land and many titles, including that of Lord of Bridestowe, a village still extant in Devon, in the west of England. Details of the grant were set forth in Doomsday Book in 1086. These titles and lands descended to Moore's ancestor, Hugh de Courtenay, Earl of Devon, who married the Conqueror's descendant, Lady Margaret de Bohun, granddaughter of King Edward I. Her dowry included Powderham Castle, perhaps England's finest castle today, still the seat of the Courtenay Earls of Devon. The Bridestowe title and land eventually passed to Moore. He had earlier been made a knight by Queen Elizabeth II, and has a coat of arms.

Baldwin's older brother, Richard, another of the Conqueror's Companions at Hastings, was created Earl of Clare. One of his descendants, Lady Elizabeth de Clare, another granddaughter of King Edward I, founded Clare College at Cambridge University. Yale University, six centuries after Clare's founding, coincidentally offered Moore, upon his graduation *magna cum laude* from Yale, two years' study at Clare College as the Yale-Clare Scholar.

Professionally, Moore has become one of New York's foremost litigators. In 2002, his best-known current case is a $100 million compensatory and punitive damage lawsuit against Columbia University. The University, as part of a ghastly experiment, fraudulently accused New York's top restaurants of poisoning one of its professors, to see how people react to having their lives destroyed. As another lawyer put it, "Now Columbia knows; people react by hiring you." The commencement of the lawsuit resulted in interviews by all 7 TV channels the first day and continuing worldwide press coverage, including a front-page article and photograph in *The New York Sun* on June 12, 2002.

Chapter 30

Willard Sean Moore, Esq. (1958–)
m. 1993*
Margaret Else Nelson, Esq. (1947–)
Elizabeth Margaret Clarissa Moore, (1960–)
Charles Ralph Henry Moore, (1963–)

This chapter remains to be written, by them.

---

* Willard married Margaret in 1993 (at St. James' Episcopal Church in New York City), echoing the marriage of Willard (King) to Margaret (Erickson) 63 years earlier and the marriage of Thomas (Moore) to Margaret (King) 38 years earlier.

Chapter 31

Sarah Elizabeth Moore, (1994–)

Even more, this chapter remains to be written, by her.

Appendix

The genealogy is as follows:

1. William the Conqueror (1027–1087) m. 1053 Matilda of Flanders (c. 1032–1083), their son
2. King Henry I (1068–1135) m. 1100 Princess Matilda of Scotland (1080–1118), their daughter was Matilda:
3. Geoffrey Plantagenet*, Count of Anjou (1113–1151) m. 1128 Matilda the Empress (c. 1102–1167), their son
4. King Henry II (1133–1189) m. 1152 Eleanor of Aquitaine (1122–1204), their son
5. King John "Lackland" (1167–1216) m. 1200 Isabella of Angoulême (c. 1187–1246), their son
6. King Henry III (1207–1272) m. 1236 Eleanor of Provence (1224–1291), their son
7. King Edward I "Longshanks" (1239–1307) m. 1254 Princess Eleanor of Castile (c. 1245–1290), their daughter was Elizabeth:
8. Humphrey de Bohun VIII, 4th Earl of Hereford and 3d Earl of Essex, Constable of England (c. 1276–1322)**, m. 1302 Her

---

* See footnote p. vii.

** The title of Viscount Hereford was held in 1990 by Robert Milo Leicester Devereux, 18th Viscount, b. 1932, residence The Lyford Cay Club. The name de Bohun is preserved in his son Hon. Charles Robin de Bohun Devereux, b. 1975. Mary de Bohun, coheiress of the Hereford earldom, married in 1380 Henry of Bolingbroke who in 1397 became Duke of Hereford and in 1399 King Henry IV of England.

Appendix

Royal Highness Princess Elizabeth Plantagenet (1282–1316), their daughter was Margaret:

9. Hugh de Courtenay, 2d Earl of Devon (1303–1377) m. 1325 Lady Margaret de Bohun (c. 1314–1391)*, their daughter was Margaret:
10. John de Cobham 3d Baron Cobham (1316–1408) m. 1332 Lady Margaret de Courtenay (c. 1326–1395), their daughter was Joane:
11. Sir John de la Pole (d. 1380) m. 1362 Lady Joane de Cobham (d. c. 1379), their daughter was Joane:
12. Sir Reginald de Braybroke, Knight Banneret (d. 1405) m. 1392 Lady Joane de la Pole (c. 1379–1434) 4th Baron(ess) Cobham in 1408, their daughter was Joane:
13. Sir Thomas Brooke (c. 1392–1439) m. 1410 Lady Joane de Braybroke (c. 1398–1442) 5th Baron(ess) Cobham in 1434, their son
14. Reginald Brooke, Esq. (b. c. 1420), younger brother of Sir Edward Brooke 6th Baron Cobham, m. Anne Evelyn, their daughter was Elizabeth:
15. Francis Peyton, Esq. m. Elizabeth Brooke, their son
16. Christopher Peyton, Esq. m. Joanne Mildmay, their son
17. Christopher Peyton, Esq., Auditor General in Ireland (d. 1612) m. 2d Alice Newman, their daughter was Anne:
18. Sir Richard Cooke, Principal Secretary of State and Chancellor of the Exchequer in Ireland (d. 1616) m. c. 1595 Anne Peyton, (c. 1576–after 1637), their son
19. William Cooke, Esq., First Master of the Dublin Goldsmiths' Company (c. 1600–1642) m. c. 1625 Lettice Fisher, their son

---

* This title continues in the Courtenay Family, with interruptions, and modifications, in 1990, with Charles Christopher Courtenay, b. 1916, as 17th Earl of Devon, Powderham Castle, near Exeter, England. Powderham Castle was part of the dowry Lady Margaret de Bohun brought to her marriage in 1325 to Hugh de Courtenay, who became 2d Earl of Devon in 1340.

Appendix

20. Arthur Cooke, Esq. (c. 1625–1682) m. c. 1655 Margaret Sacheverell, their son
21. Walsingham Cooke, Esq. (c. 1660–1724) m. 1698 Anne Bower, their daughter was Frances:
22. Frederick? Proctor m. c. 1738 Frances Cooke (c. 1713–?), their daughter was Frances:
23. William Moore (c. 1740–c. 1820) m. c. 1766 Frances Proctor (c. 1741–before 1817), their son
24. Walsingham Moore, gentleman (1768–1871) m. 1805 his first cousin Frances Proctor (1783–1867) widow of O'Connor, their son
25. Mark Moore (1820–1890) m. 1843 in Canada Anne Elliott (1826–1903), their son
26. W(alsingham) Proctor Moore (1847–1902) m. c. 1869 Fanny Gillon (1848–1881), their son
27. Ralph Henry Moore, Sr. (1873–1945) m. 1907 in the U. S. Blanche Eloise Rosenwater (1880–1964), their son
28. Ralph Henry (Jack) Moore, Jr. (1909–1980) m. 1930 Estelle Marguerite Hero (1911–1968), their son
29. Thomas R(onald) Moore, Esq. (1932–   ) m. 1955 Margaret Clarissa King (1932–   ), their children
30. Willard Sean Moore, Esq. (1958–   ) m. 1993 Margaret Else Nelson, Esq. (1947–   ) their daughter is named below; Elizabeth Margaret Clarissa Moore, (1960–   ); Charles Ralph Henry Moore, (1963–   )
31. Sarah Elizabeth Moore, (1994–   )

Notes

Works not cited in full below are set forth in the Selected Bibliography, which follows.

Dramatis Personae

1. Sir Francis Walsingham was also a direct ancestor of Queen Elizabeth II, because his female descendants married so well:

    His daughter Frances Walsingham married the favorite of Elizabeth I: Robert Devereux 2d Earl of Essex. Their daughter Frances Devereux married William Seymour 2d Duke of Somerset. Their daughter Jane Seymour married Charles Boyle Viscount Dungarvon and produced a line of Earls. Their great-granddaughter Charlotte Boyle Baroness Clifford married William Cavendish 4th Duke of Devonshire. Their daughter Lady Dorothy Cavendish married William Henry Bentinck 3d Duke of Portland, and their third son, Lord William Charles Augustus Cavendish-Bentinck, married Anne Wellesley, daughter of the above-mentioned Richard Colley Wellesley Marquess Wellesley, who was a principal architect of the British Empire in India. Anne Wellesley's great-great-granddaughter became Queen Elizabeth II.

    In the issue of the marriage of Anne Wellesley, the bloodlines of Sir Francis Walsingham and Anne Peyton merged.

Chapter 2

2. Wier, pp. 48–49.

Chapter 4

3. IX D.N.B. 456.

Notes

Chapter 7

4. Wier, pp. 73, 80–81.

Chapter 8

5. Sir Anthony Wagner, English Genealogy (3d ed. 1983), pp. 235–236.

Chapter 9

6. All dates except 1314 are from Burke's Peerage, p. 791. The 1314 date is from Weir, p. 84.
7. K. B. McFarlane, The Nobility of Late Medieval England (1973), pp. 143–144.
8. Gies, p. 78.
9. IV D.N.B. 1269.
10. Letter to author from Col. Cedric Delforce, Courtenay Archivist, Powderham Castle, Exeter EX6 8JQ, England, 4 January 1994, telephone 011–44–626–890252.

Chapter 10

11. Booklet "The Brasses" published by the Church of St. Mary Magdalene, Cobham, co. Kent, England (c. 1986), p. 4.
12. Burke's Peerage, p. 791.
13. IV D.N.B. 612.
14. Hasted, 3 History of Kent 409.
15. 109 Kent 329.
16. An article describing the castle in detail is in 11 Kent 128–144 with a 1991 update in 109 Kent 329–330.
17. The Brasses, p. 4.
18. 11 Kent 49–59. An interesting interlock of history is that the Scots Queen in 1314 would be exchanged for Earl Humphrey de Bohun whose granddaughter would marry the grandson of the 1st Baron Cobham.
19. 84 Kent 211–229.

Notes

Chapter 11

20. Contract 21 October 1362; Horrox, p. 34; Burke's Peerage, p. 591; IV D.N.B. 612.
21. Horrox, p. 22.
22. XIV D.N.B. 981.
23. Harvey, p. 58, cited in Horrox.
24. Horrox, p. 8.
25. Horrox, p. 11.
26. Court of Chancery, Close Rolls 1360–1364, pp. 425–427.
27. Horrox, p. 33.
28. On 26 June 1366; his uncle died five days earlier, on 21 June 1366. XVI D.N.B. 49; Horrox, p. 25.
29. Horrox, p. 43.
30. Court of Chancery, Close Rolls 1349–1354, p. 608.
31. The local historian in the village of Chrishall is the delightful elderly Irene Cranwell, Faerie Cottage, Chrishall near Royston, Herts SG8 8QN, England.
32. R.R. Sharpe, ed., 2 Calendar of Wills Proved and Enrolled in the Court of Husting, London, 1258–1688 (1890), p. 215.
33. 18 Ency. Brit. 148 (1970).
34. Court of Chancery, Close Rolls 1377–1381, p. 370.
35. Court of Chancery, Patent Rolls 1377–1381, pp. 518, 567.

Chapter 12

36. Paget Q118857.
37. Burke, Dormant Peerages, pp. 464*, 32.
38. Gies, pp. 196–197.
39. XIV D.N.B. 981.
40. Court of Chancery, Close Rolls 1377–1381, p. 370.
41. Burke's Peerage, p. 591, Burke, Dormant Peerages, p. 125.
42. Court of Chancery, Close Rolls 1377–1381, pp. 511–512.
43. 3 Cokayne 345.
44. Court of Chancery, Close Rolls 1389–1392, p. 434.

Notes

45. W. Pritchett, Cobham (1993), p. 6. Available from Mr. Pritchett in Cobham.
46. The Brasses, p. 6.
47. XIV D.N.B. 981.
48. Burke's Peerage, p. 591, XIV D.N.B. 986.
49. She had arranged the marriage of this daughter, Lady Joane de Braybroke, aged about 12, to Sir Thomas Brooke of Brooke, Somerset, in 1410. This daughter succeeded to the title in 1434. Neither this daughter nor her husband lived to see their oldest son, Sir Edward Brooke, called to Parliament in 1445 by King Henry VI as the 6th Baron Cobham, reviving the barony in terms of parliamentary representation.

    Confusion is caused by the fact that some authorities would count him as the 4th Baron, ignoring his grandmother and mother who were the 4th and 5th Baron(esse)s. Burke's Peerage, the D.N.B. and I count him as the 6th Baron. Burke's Peerage, p. 521, XIX D.N.B. 518.

    His mother of course could never live to see him called to Parliament as Lord *Cobham*.

Chapter 13

50. Furnivall, p. 138.
51. *Ibid*.
52. 3 Cokayne 346, Burke's Peerage, p. 591 and Paget P59429.
53. 11 Kent 101.
54. See Burke's Landed Gentry, 1952 ed., p. 274. Holditch is 4 miles NE of Axminster. Ilchester and Holditch are about 20 miles apart.
55. Furnivall, pp. 26–28.
56. See will and Paget Q118857.
57. Blue Guide Churches and Chapels, p. 185.
58. Text of will from Furnivall, pp. 129–130.
59. Hasted, 3 History of Kent 412.

Notes

Chapter 14
60. Burke's Peerage, p. 591.
61. XIX D.N.B. 1003.
62. 11 Kent 103.
63. 3 Cokayne 346.
64. Burke's Peerage, pp. 591–592.
65. Burke, Dormant Peerages, p. 76, Burke's Landed Gentry, 1952 ed., p. 274.

Chapter 15
66. Paget Q118849, Q118850.
67. Burke, Dormant Peerages, pp. 76–77.

Chapter 16
68. Stanford E. Lehmberg, Sir Walter Mildmay and Tudor Government (1964), H. A. St. John Mildmay, A Brief Memoir of the Mildmay Family (1913), Paget N14859/60, XIII D.N.B. 374, G.O. 178 p. 236.

Chapter 17
69. Calendar of State Papers, Ireland, 1581, p. 335.
70. Calendar, 1584, p. 530.
71. Calendar, 1585, p. 586.
72. Calendar, 1589, p. 125.
73. Calendar, 1595, p. 340.
74. Calendar, 1597, p. 233.
75. Calendar, 1586, p. 103.
76. Calendar, 1600, pp. 304–5.
77. His 1611 report, in 6 Carew 179.
78. XV D.N.B. 1020.
79. Paget L3716.

Chapter 18
80. College of Arms, London.
81. For the dates see Paget. A second daughter of Edward Lewknor, Alice, married Walter Moore, ancestor of Viscount

Notes

Garret Moore of Drogheda. Anne, Countess of Drogheda, History of the Moore Family (1902), pp. 2–3.
82. Sir Anthony Wagner, English Genealogy, p. 280.
83. 3 Carew 220–260.
84. Calendar of State Papers, Ireland, 1603, pp. 207, 277.
85. Auditor Peyton's 1611 report, in 6 Carew 179, 182, 184.
86. 4 Carew 433–434.
87. Calendar of State Papers, Ireland, 1613, p. 452.
88. John O'Hart, The Irish and Anglo-Irish Landed Gentry (1884, 1968), p. 228. Also listed is Sir Edward Fisher's father, Capt. Henry Fisher, and Lt. John Fisher.
89. 6 Carew 301.
90. 6 Carew 312.
91. 6 Carew 327.
92. XX D.N.B. 1121.
93. 8 Kildare 371.
94. R.C. Simington, ed., Irish Manuscripts Commission, VIII Civil Survey 1654 (1952), p. 178.
95. XX D.N.B. 1121.
96. 8 Kildare 371.
97. Paget.
98. Anne, Countess of Drogheda, History of the Moore Family, *supra*, at pp. 46, 162A.
99. XIII D.N.B. 793, 797.
100. Paget. Paget lists Anne Peyton K1858, Dudley Colley J929, Henry Colley I465, Richard Colley H233, Garret Wellesley G117, Richard Colley Wellesley F59, Anne Wellesley E30, Charles W. F. Cavendish-Bentinck D15, Nina Cecilia Cavendish-Bentinck C8, Lady Elizabeth Bowes-Lyon B4, Queen Elizabeth II A2.

Chapter 19

101. 6 Carew 383.

Notes

102. Parish Register Society of Dublin, Registers of St. John the Evangelist 1619 to 1699 (1906), lists "8 June 1620 chrisnd Elizabeth Cooke dau. to Walsingham Cooke [niece of William Cooke]" (p. 3), the 1621 church assessment of Sir Edward Fisher, kt., of Fishamble Street (p. 273), and the burial of William Cooke on 17 September 1642 (p. 48). The P.R.S. records are in the care of Church of Ireland, Representative Church Body Library, Braemor Park, Rathgar, Dublin 14, Ireland.
103. 3 Carew 257–258, 4 Carew 116, 6 Carew 383, 6 Carew 187, 6 Carew 211, 6 Carew 324, 4 Carew 262, 4 Carew 368.
104. Burke, General Armory (1969 ed.), p. 351 and entries Fisher and Giggins.
105. Id. at 352.
106. IV D.N.B. 232.
107. Sir Charles J. Jackson, F.S.A., English Goldsmiths and Their Marks (2d ed. 1921, 1964), pp. 565–575, 606, 626, 633, 634, 667.
108. Royal Society of Antiquaries of Ireland, Journal, 1912, p. 163.
109. Philip H. Hore, 6 History of Wexford (1911) pp. 467–68. Calendar of State Papers, Ireland, 1620, entry Walsingham Cooke. G.O. 178, p. 235. Hore, vol. 6, p. 644.
110. Association for Preservation of Memorials of Dead in Ireland, Journal, vol. 1, 1891, pp. 517–19 (NY Public Library Genealogy Room); Burke's Peerage, entry Parsons.
111. R.C. Simington, ed., Irish Manuscripts Commission, IX Civil Survey 1654 (1953), pp. 23, 24, 38, 39, 40, 42, 59.
112. Association Journal cited above.
113. XIII D.N.B. 790.
114. Hore, vol. 6, pp. 478, 652; vol. 4, p. 57.
115. Hore, vol. 4, p. 63.
116. Burke's General Armory (1969 ed.), p. 352.
117. Hore, vol. 6, pp. 150, 589; Burke's, p. 225.

Notes

118. Letter to author from Lancaster Herald dtd 2 February 1994; G.O. 178, p. 235.

Chapter 20

119. R.C. Simington, ed., Irish Manuscripts Commission, IX Civil Survey 1654 (1953), p. 55.
120. John O'Hart, The Irish and Anglo-Irish Landed Gentry (1884, 1969) p. 228. Hore, vol. 6, p. 280; vol. 4, p. 329.
121. G.O. 178, p. 235, and Pole-Hore Mss., vol. 38, p. 135, in St. Peter's College, Wexford.
122. G.O. 205, p. 354.

Chapter 21

123. Paul Johnson, Ireland (1980), pp. 56–57. Peter Berresford Ellis, Hell or Connaught: the Cromwellian Colonisation of Ireland, 1652–1660 (1975).
124. One of the devastating facts of life is that most Irish original records were destroyed by Irish cannonading and the resultant fires in the rebellion of 1922.
125. John O'Hart, The Irish and Anglo-Irish Landed Gentry; John O'Hart, Irish Pedigrees; John P. Prendergast, The Cromwellian Settlement of Ireland.
126. Paul Johnson, Ireland, p. 61.
127. Phyllis Deane, The First Industrial Revolution (1965), pp. 8–9.
128. 9 Kildare 50, 186.
129. G.O. 178, p. 235, and Pole-Hore Mss., both cited above.
130. O'Hart, cited above. See also Paul Johnson, Ireland, p. 62.

Chapter 22

131. 9 Kildare 50, 186.
132. G.O. 178, p. 235, and Pole-Hore Mss, both cited above.
133. Wm. Proctor Moore, son of John Moore b. 1852, son of Walsingham Proctor Moore b. 1808, son of Walsingham Moore b. 1768, told Edw. F. Moore that William Moore b. c.

Notes

1740 "married Frances Proctor whose father, first name unknown to him, was employed in the Customs Service."

134. He married for the second time, probably in 1811, and had a son in 1814, when he would have been 60 and 63, respectively, if born in 1751.

Chapter 23

135. Lecky, p. 470.
136. Letter to author from Church of Ireland, Representative Church Body Library, Braemor Park, Rathgar, Dublin 14, Ireland, dtd 8 July 1993.
137. A. L. Rowse, The England of Elizabeth (1950), p. 231.
138. George Taylor, History of the Rebellion in County Wexford (3d ed. 1829) pp. 128–129, lists Daniel Moore as among the 37 loyalists killed on that date in that encounter. Also, statement of Isabella Moore Ross to Edw. F. Moore in 1941 as to Daniel's death.
139. A letter of Daniel Moore of Dublin, son of William, to his uncle Walsingham in Ontario, dated 20 April 1819, indicates that Margaret and Anne were then in Canada and that Margaret then had children.
140. Kee, pp. 59–65.
141. Written statement of his grandson in 1908.
142. Lecky, p. 367.
143. IV Lecky, p. 344.
144. Kee, p. 65.
145. Sir Richard Musgrave, Memoirs of Rebellions in Ireland, vol. 2, p. 206 (3d ed. 1802).
146. *Id.* at App. XIX, 9 p. 356, which also lists "some [about 1,000] of the protestants massacred in the diocese of Ferns and county of Wexford," but not Daniel Moore. But see Taylor, *supra*, for a listing of Daniel Moore as being killed on 22 June 1798.
147. V Lecky, p. 359.

Notes

148. This U. K. peerage was extinguished in 1892 but was "recreated" in this branch of the Moore line in 1954 with Baron Moore of Cobham, Surrey. This village of Cobham is 30 miles W of the village of Cobham in Kent where lived the Lords Cobham.

149. Vol. XIII, no. 32, Tuesday, 12 August 1817, p. 255.

150. West half of Lot 17, 8th Concession, County of Leeds, Township of Yonge, and East half of Lot 17, respectively, R.G. 1, Quarter-Master General's List of Emigrants (1815–1822), p. 21, Archives Toronto, which also lists their arrival on "Mary Ann 8 August 1817" by "Consent of the Forces."

151. Statement of Isabella Moore Ross to Edw. F. Moore in 1941.

Chapter 24

152. Written statement of Walsingham's grandson William Moore son of Mark Moore on 7 October 1937: "Grand Father and Grand Mother were both born in Dublin, Ireland [and] were highly educated. Grand Father had some office under George III." Ltr. to Edw. F. Moore.

153. Four factors argue for Walsingham Moore's being born in 1768. First, his tombstone says he was aged 103 when he died in 1871. Second, he was probably born before Frederick's birth in 1770 because his uncle Walsingham Proctor was a dominant factor in the Moore family life, and it would be likely that the earlier-born of these two sons would be named "Walsingham." Third, the tradition was to name the second son for the mother's father and Frederick Moore was probably named for his mother's father Frederick? Proctor. Fourth, a newspaper account refers to his 100th birthday, p. 159. The birth year 1774 is argued for by the 1861 census. It lists him as 87 (not 93). But that census was inaccurate. It incorrectly listed the family as "Moor," Anne Elliott Moore as "Ann," and her age as "33" instead of "35." Query whether that census arbitrarily listed Walsingham as 10 years older than his wife.

Notes

154. Written statement of Frederick's grandson in 1908: "Frederick Moore, Sr., was born in Dublin, Ireland, in the year 1770."
155. Note 152.
156. Great Britain Parliament Sessional Papers 1837, vol. XI, Pt. 2, p. 137 (Readex Fiche 06024). As noted, members of the Guilds could vote for members of Parliament, which inspired the 1837 parliamentary inquiry. "Grace Especial" was under special attack although it had been rare and in 1837 was nonexistent.
157. Statement of his granddaughter Mrs. Isabella Moore Ross, daughter of Mark Moore, to Edw. F. Moore on July 14, 1941.
158. Besides the Minute Books, G.B.P.S.P., 1837, vol. XI, Pt. 2, App. No. 3, p. 162 (Readex Fiche 06027), lists members admitted after 1792. See also ltr. of Mr. Sadleir of G.O. Dublin to Edw. F. Moore, 14 June 1937.
159. Also, Wm. Moore's 1937 ltr. stated, "Grand Mother's name was Frances Proctor."
160. Kee, p. 69.
161. VI D.N.B. 780.
162. Lecky, p. 479.
163. 10 Kildare 83, 90.
164. Philip Guedalla, Wellington (1931), p. 136.
165. Lease between George Story of Fade (?) Dublin, Peace Officer, and Walsingham Proctor, of South Frederick St., Dublin, gt. Said Story for the consideration of £26.3.3d to him in hand paid by said Proctor as a fine [a conveyancing term] and also for and in consideration of the yearly rent and costs herein and therein mentioned set all that plot of ground, situate in Eastmoreland Park in said city, containing in front to Hobart's Passage 42 feet and in breadth in the rere or on the east 27 feet, bounded in the said rere by a garden of said Hobart, containing in depth on the south and bounded by William Chapman's lot, 93 feet 6 inches, with the dwelling

Notes

house and all other buildings now built thereon. To hold said premises with appurtenances to said Proctor from 29 September next for 58 years to be computed from 29 March last and to be from thenceforth rent ensuing fully to be completed and ended, at the yearly rent of £26.3.3d payable by four equal quarterly payments above taxes.

Deed and memorial are witnessed by Jas. Kildahl and Walsingham Moore, both of Dublin, gt.

   Sworn 5th Aug. 1806.   *George Story*
   (585.79.394591)

166. R.G.1, Quarter-Master General's List of Emigrants (1815–1822), p. 21, Archives Toronto, would list Walsingham Moore as having emigrated to Canada from Ireland in 1817 with his wife and five children, ages—presumably in 1822: one male child over 12 (Walsingham Proctor Moore, born 1808), two male children under 12 (William, born 1811, and Frederick, born 1815), and two female children over 12 (therefore born between 1806 and 1810).

167. Deed between Walsingham Proctor, of Dublin, gt. and Wm. Moore of sd city, gt. Whereby in consideration of the sum of £170 [I believe that the copyist erred and that this figure should be £17 since the annual rent was £16] to be paid to him in manner therein mentd he sd Proctor did demise to sd Moore that lot of ground situate in Eastmoreland Park, containing in the front and in breadth to Hobart's passage 42 ft and in breadth in the rere or on the east 27 ft; bounded on the sd rere by a garden of sd Hobart, containing in depth on the south and bounded by Wm. Chapman's lot (93 ft 6 ins, with the dwelling house and all other buildings now built thereon as the same were formerly demised by Patrick Dowling to Geo. Storey and by sd Storey to sd Proctor. To hold from 24th June then inst for 53 yrs to be computed from 29th March then last, at the yearly rent of £16 payable quarterly above taxes.

Notes

Witnessed by Bernard McDonald and Henry Carrell, both of sd city, gt.

Walsingham Proctor

- - - - - - - delivered sd deed and this memorial to Oliver Moore, Esq. Dept Regr on 3rd Jany 1816.

Regd 3rd Jany 1816
(697.96.478240.)

168. According to Mrs. Ross's 1941 statement, Walsingham Moore declined his father-in-law's offer of a job in Dublin, which offer was latter accepted by Walsingham Moore's brother. Writing to Walsingham Moore in Canada on April 20, 1819, Daniel, son of Walsingham Moore's brother, William Moore, referred to "my father, William Moore, Stamp Office, Dublin." We also know that "William Moore was employed [in 1829] as a fourth Stamper in the Stamp Office, Ireland." Ltr. to Edw. F. Moore from Secretaries Office, Inland Revenue, Somerset House, London, W.C., 2, Oct. 31, 1951.

169. Johnson, The Birth of the Modern, pp. 203–206.

170. 17 Ency. Brit. 519 (1970); Kee, p. 78.

171. Grun, Timetables of History 385 (1975).

172. East half of Lot 17, 8th Concession, County of Leeds, Township of Yonge, and west half of Lot 17, respectively, R.G. 1, Quarter-Master General's List of Emigrants (1815–1822), p. 21, Archives Toronto, which also lists their arrival on "Mary Ann 8 August 1817" by "Consent of the Forces."

Chapter 25

173. Letter of grandson, Ralph Henry Moore, Sr., dtd 2 October 1939.

As we have seen, the ship itself sailed from Wexford.

174. Frances Jane Moore married her second cousin, John Francis Moore, grandson of Frederick Moore (who had come to Leeds Co., Ontario, from Ireland in 1811) and Eliza Bolton, and son of William Moore and Deborah Ann Francis. Frances

Notes

and John had a son Dr. Mark Hilton Ponsonby Moore. In 1892 in the U. K., the family's distant cousin, William Ponsonby Moore, succeeded *his* distant cousin Henry Francis Moore as 9th Earl of Drogheda (the Marquessate expiring on the death of Henry Francis Moore). The Moores in Canada were aware that their ancestor Walsingham Moore who came to Canada in 1817, and therefore they themselves, were related to the Marquesses (1791–1892) and Earls of Drogheda (1661–present). The name "Ponsonby" in connection with the Moore families goes back to the marriage in 1727 of Lady Sarah Ponsonby (daughter of the Earl of Bessborough) to Edward Moore, 5th Earl of Drogheda.

175. Enum. Dist. 3 folio (page) 76 of 79, entries #18–29, on microfilm, Archives Ottawa.

Chapter 26

176. First child born in 1844 (Ann's 1908 Duluth probate).
177. Obit and gravestone: d. 1881, aged 33; Death Cert.: b. Canada.
178. A much larger town than Athens, 10 miles south of Athens, on the St. Lawrence River. Doubtless named for Sir Isaac Brock, Lt. Governor and Commander-in-Chief of Upper Canada in the Canadian-U. S. Border Skirmishes of 1812.
179. Obit in unidentified newspaper.
180. Frances Jane Moore had married her second cousin, John Francis Moore, grandson of Frederick Moore (who had come to Leeds Co., Ontario, from Ireland in 1811) and Eliza Bolton, and son of William Moore and Deborah Ann Francis. They had three children of their own when Fanny Gillon Moore died: Williametta Moore, b. 1866, m. Herbert Hull, d. 2 September 1909; Dr. Mark Hilton Ponsonby Moore, b. 19 April 1873, m. Annis Jackson, d. 26 May 1941; and Lorne Bruce Moore, the Reeve, b. 1880, m. Alma Cheetham, alive in 1957.
181. The column wrongly lists "Proctor W." instead of "W. Proctor," a not surprising error by the stonecutter since the use

Notes

of a first initial is uncommon in North America while common in Britain. His son always referred to him as "W. Proctor," or "Proctor" or "W. P.," as do all family records.

Chapter 27
182. Annual Duluth Directories and Ann's Duluth Death Certificate and probate papers.
183. Death Certificate.
184. Obit in unidentified Kennett newspaper in 1933.

Chapter 29
185. XX Dictionary of American Biography (1936) p. 240.
186. XIII D.N.B. 912.

Selected Bibliography

Sir William Betham, Ulster King of Arms, Registered Pedigree of William Cooke, G.O. 178, pp. 234–237, 16 October 1849. (Earlier, G.O. 205, pp. 350–355.) Genealogical Office, 2 Kildare Street, Dublin 2, Ireland.

Blue Guide Churches and Chapels Southern England (1st ed. 1991), Blue Guide England (10th ed. 1989), Blue Guide Ireland (6th ed. 1992), WW Norton & Co.

Sir Bernard Burke, Ulster King of Arms, Dormant and Extinct Peerages (1883, reprinted 1962).

Burke's Peerage and Baronetage (1975 ed.).

Church of St. Mary Magdalene, Cobham, Kent, England, The Brasses (c. 1986).

G.E. Cokayne, Complete Peerage, 13 vols. (1910–1940).

Debrett's Peerage and Baronetage (1990 ed.).

Dictionary of National Biography (D.N.B.) XXII vols. (1900, reprinted in 1922).

F.J. Furnivall, ed., Early English Text Society, Fifty Earliest English Wills, original series No. 78 (1882, reprinted 1964).

Joseph & Frances Gies, Life in a Medieval Castle (1974).

Rosemary Horrox, The de la Poles of Hull, East Yorkshire Local History Series, no. 38 (1983).

Paul Johnson, The Birth of the Modern (1991).

Robert Kee, Ireland (1982).

Kent Archaeological Society, Archaeologia Cantiana, especially vol. 11 (1877), J.G. Waller, The Lords of Cobham, Their Monuments, and the Church, pp. 49–112; Coulyng Castle, pp. 128–144; vol. 84 (1969), Estates of the Cobham Family

Selected Bibliography

in the Later Thirteenth Century, pp. 211–229, cited as (volume) Kent (page).

Kildare Archaeological Society, Journal, cited as (volume) Kildare (page).

W. E. H. Lecky, History of Ireland, V vols. (1893), 1 vol. (1972).

Gerald Paget, The Lineage & Ancestry of H.R.H. Prince Charles, Prince of Wales, 2 vols. (1977).

Totnes, George Carew, 1st earl of, Calendar of Carew Manuscripts, 6 vols., cited as (volume) Carew (page).

Alison Weir, Britain's Royal Families (1989).

Key Sources

The source of this genealogy is the Registered Pedigree of William Cooke, compiled and certified on 16 October 1849 by Sir William Betham, Ulster King of Arms. It is countersigned by Sir J. Bernard Burke who succeeded Sir William as Ulster King of Arms in 1853. The Pedigree is in G.O. 178, pp. 234–237 (with an earlier work in G.O. 205, pp. 350–355) in the Genealogical Office, 2 Kildare Street, Dublin 2, Ireland. The focus of the Pedigree compiled by Sir William is on Sir Richard Cooke (d. 1616), son of William Cooke, and on Sir Richard's wife, Anne Peyton. Anne Peyton's ancestry is traced back to King Edward I of England, and her progeny are traced forward through three of her children: Sir Walsingham Cooke, William Cooke, Esq., and Dudley Colley, Esq. One can assume that the original interest was in tracing the genealogy of the great Duke of Wellington and his brother the Marquess Wellesley, Lord Lieutenant of Ireland, both descended from Anne Peyton.

The seminal source in the field is the monumental life work of Gerald Paget, The Lineage and Ancestry of H.R.H. Prince Charles, Prince of Wales, 2 vols. (1977). In it Paget traces the ancestry of Prince Charles back through Anne Peyton (#18 in this genealogy, #K1856 in his) and others to generation #10 in this genealogy. He confirms Betham in every important respect and supplies a wealth of dates. Biographies of the first 12 generations are set out in the 22 volumes of the Dictionary of National Biography (1900, reprinted in 1922), as well as in Betham's Registered Pedigree of William Cooke*.

---

* The immediate provenance of this Registered Pedigree can be surmised: John Henry O'Byrne Redmond (great-grandson of John Cooke,

Key Sources

Esq., the brother of Frances Cooke Proctor, generation #22 in this genealogy) married Emelia Georgiana Manley, daughter of General Count Manley, on 22 September 1849, shortly before Sir William Betham certified this pedigree on 16 October 1849, their marriage being the last entry. An earlier identical pedigree was complied by Sir William Betham and is in G.O. 205, pp. 350–355, from volume 3 of Will Pedigrees. From this marriage, celebrated at Alton Towers seat of the Earl of Shrewsbury, Reginald Pius Rudolph Plantagenet Redmond was born in 1851; he succeeded his father in 1866 as Count of the Papal States and inherited Sleanagrane (Cookestowne) co. Wexford. John O'Hart, Irish Pedigrees (1892, 5th ed. 1976), p. 366.

Index

Women are generally listed under their maiden name.

Abigail 190
Addison, Ontario 155
Adele, daughter of William the Conqueror 4, 18
Adele, of Vermandois 6
Agamain, Charles 192
Aldington 55
Alexander the Great 14
Alfred, brother of Edward the Confessor 2, 3
Alfred the Great, King 7, 17
Alice, Princess betrothed to Richard Lionheart 23
American Civil War 154
American Lawyer 194
American Revolution 154
Andover 195
Anglo-Irish Ascendancy 112, 113, 133, 135, 136, 140, 150
Anglo-Saxon Chronicle 3, 14
Anjou, France 14, 23, 25
Aparias, Austria-Hungary 169
Aquitaine, Duchy of 21
Archbishop of Canterbury 22
Arklow 137

Arlette 1
Armagh, County 111
Ashington, Somerset 106
Aspall, Suffolk 83, 85
Aston's Quay 145
Athens, Ontario, Canada 142, 154, 157, 160, 163, 164, 165, 167, 168, 218
Athlone 111
Avignon 53, 62
Avon Products Inc. 193
Azusa, California 164, 168

Bachelor Girls Club 168
Bagenal, Henry 112
Ballaghkeen, Co. Wexford [Ireland] 119, 126
  Yeoman Infantry 148, 149, 153, 178
Ballyboy 127
Ballyknockane, Co. Wexford [Ireland] 126, 127
Bantry, Munster 136
Baptist, Peter, als Castilion 103
Barber-Surgeons: see Guild
Bardak, Tom 177

225

Index

Baron Cobham, see Cobham
Baron Courtenay, see
  Courtenay
Baronet, title of 103
Barry, — (Capt.) 141
Battle of the Boyne 128
Beauchamp 67
Beauchamp, Joane 51
Bec 18
Becket 20, 22
Beckley 55
Bedford, Earl of 67, 106
Belfast, Ireland 116, 136
Benenden, Kent 111
Bentinck, William Henry 205
Berkeley 195
Bermuda 190
Bernard, King of Italy 6
  Margaret 85, 86
Bessborough, Earl of 218
Betham, William, Sir xiii,
  126, 131, 223
Beverly, Massachusetts 190
Birne, Luke 121
Black, — 169
  Adolf 170
  Betty 170
  Fannie 170
  Leopold 170
  Sarah 169, 170, 172
Blackwater, Ulster 112
Blore Heath 82
Blount, Charles (Lord
  Mountjoy) 93, 95, 107,
  112, 113
Bohun, de

Arms 35, 43
Henry, 1st Earl of Hereford, signer of Magna Carta 25, 42, 196
Humphrey I, Baron 7, 41
  III, Baron 41, 42
  V, 2d Earl of Hereford, 1st Earl of Essex 30, 42
  VI 30
  VIII, 4th Earl of Hereford, 3d Earl of Essex 7, 41, 42, 60, 202, 206
Margaret, Lady (married Hugh de Courtenay, 2d Earl of Devon) 42, 45, 46, 51, 202
Mary, Lady 43, 201
Bolingbroke, Henry 43, 68
Bolton, — 128, 138
  Eliza 135, 141, 151, 217
  Elizabeth 218
  John 129
Boroughbridge, Yorkshire 42
Bourchier, George 106
Bourney, H. G. 153
Bower, Anne 127, 128, 131, 203
Bowes-Lyon, Elizabeth 111, 210
Boyle, Charles 205
  Charlotte 205
Braybroke, de
  Arms 66, 72
  Elizabeth 82
  Gerard 67, 82
  Henry 67

226

Index

Joane, 5th Baroness Cobham 69, 73, 79, 81, 202, 208
Reginald, Sir 65, 67, 68, 69, 71, 79, 82, 202
Reginald 68, 79
Robert 68, 79
Bristol 73
Brittany 25
Brockville, Ontario [Canada] 158, 164, 167, 168, 172
Brooke
Anne (Evelyn) 83, 86, 202
Arms 66, 72
Edward, 6th Baron Cobham 80, 81, 82, 86, 202, 208
Elizabeth 83, 85, 86, 91, 202
John 81, 86
Reginald 80, 81, 83, 86, 202
Somerset 208
Thomas (3 generations) 73–81, 202, 208
Brown, E. (Mrs.) 165
Bruges 53
Brunham 68
Bryan, James 121, 122
Buckingham Palace 51
Burgh, Lord 107, 112
Burghley, Lord 90, 92, 101, 102
Burgoyne, Grace 85
John 85
Bury St. Edmunds, Suffolk 85, 86, 91, 101, 105
Caen 5

Cairo, Illinois 168, 169, 170, 175
Cambridge 62
Cambridge, Massachusetts 191
Cambridge University 91, 92, 189
Camden, William 109, 116
Canada 105, 132, 141, 142, 143, 150, 151, 152, 153, 159, 167, 171, 203, 216, 217, 218
Canute, King 2, 3
Carbury, Co. Kildare [Ireland] 110
Carew, George 112
Carey, John 92
Carleton Place, Ontario 162, 163, 164
Carrell, Henry 217
Castile 37
Castle Ashby 67
Castle Carbury, Co. Kildare [Ireland] 109, 110, 111, 121
Castle-Ellish, Barony of Ballaghkeen 127
Parish of 126
Cavendish, Dorothy 205
William 205
Cavendish-Bentinck, Charles W. F. 111, 210
Nina Cecilia 111, 210
William Charles Augustus 205
Cecil, Robert 102, 107
William 92, 93

Index

Chaîne des Rôtisseurs 194
Chapman, William 215, 216
Chara: see Hero
Charlemagne xiii, 2, 5, 6, 7, 17, 195
Charles, Prince 105, 111
Charles I, King 117, 121
Charles II, King 120
Charles Martel, the Hammer 5
Chase Manhattan Bank 192
Chaucer, Geoffrey 53
Cheddar, Robert 73
Cheetham, Alma 218
Chelmsford, Essex 91
Cherd 73
Chicago, Illinois 176, 189, 191
Chichester, Arthur 113, 116
　Edward 116
　John 122
Chrishall, Essex 62, 63, 67, 79
Church of St. Mary Magdalene, Cobham, Kent, England 49, 51, 54, 65, 66, 68, 69, 71, 81
Cinque Ports 53
Cintas, Oscar B. 192
Clarendon 22
Clay, Lucius 193
Cleveland 169, 170
Cobham [Co. Kent, England] 51, 53, 54, 55, 56, 63, 69, 71, 72, 74, 79, 80, 81, 86, 206, 214
Cobham, de
　1st Baron 46, 55, 56, 206
　2d Baron 51
　3d Baron 46, 49, 51, 53, 54, 56, 61, 63, 68, 69, 202, 206
　4th Baroness 66, 67, 68, 69, 70, 71, 202
　5th Baroness 73, 79, 80, 202
　6th Baron 80, 81, 82, 83
　7th Baron 81
　Henry 54
　Joane, Lady (married de la Pole) 53, 58, 59, 61, 62, 66, 67, 71, 202
　John the Elder 55
　John the Younger 55, 56
　Lords 109
　Serlo 54
College of Arms 39, 85, 98, 103, 181, 195, 212
Colley 105, 128
　Dudley 110, 111, 121, 210
　Henry 106, 109, 110, 111, 117, 210
　Mary 110, 111
　Richard 111, 210
Comstock, H. M. 158
Conan, Duke of Brittany 6
Concord, Massachusetts 190
Connaught, Province of 95, 107
Connecticut College for Women 191
Cooke, — 128
　Anne 129
　Arthur 118, 120, 121, 122, 125, 126, 127, 128, 203
　Elizabeth 106, 119, 122, 125, 211

Index

Frances 129, 131, 132, 133, 203
Henry 129
Jane 129, 131
John 129, 131
Peyton 109, 119
Richard, Sir xiii, xv, xvi, 90, 92, 95, 98, 102, 103, 105–113, 115, 116, 119, 120, 195, 202
Thomas 119
Walsingham, Sir 106, 109, 110, 118, 119, 120, 121, 122, 125, 126, 127, 128, 129, 131, 132, 154, 203, 211
William 92, 99, 105, 109, 113, 115, 117–122, 128, 202, 211
Cookestowne, Co. Wexford [Ireland] 129, 133
Cooling Castle 52, 53, 55, 69, 70
Cornwall 45, 91
Coruna, Spain 150
Cotteleygh 73
Count of Anjou 18
Courtenay, de 116
　Arms 36, 47, 72
　Charles Christopher, 17th Earl of Devon 47, 202
　Edward, 3d Earl of Devon and Earl Marshall 46
　Hugh, Baron and 1st Earl of Devon 42, 45, 56
　Hugh, 2d Earl of Devon 42, 45, 46, 51, 202
　Margaret, Lady (married John, 3d Baron Cobham) 45, 50, 51, 53, 61, 67, 202
　Renaud 47
　William, Archbishop of Canterbury 46
Courtown 122
Cowling 52, 53
Cranwell, Irene 207
Cristeshale 62
Cromwell, Oliver 121
Cromwellian Settlements 129
Crosby, Ontario 158
Crysteshale 63
Cullentra, Parish of Monamolin 154
Cullintra, Co. Wexford [Ireland] 153
Cumbria 38
Customs Service 131, 133

Dante 31
Darnley, Earls of 55
Dartmouth 195
de Beauchamp, Richard 82
　William 82
de Burgh, Richard, 4th Earl of Clanricard 95
　Ulick, Marquis of Clanricard 95
de Floris, Pierre 47
de Hemenhale, Ralph 68
de la Pole, Arms 66, 71, 72
de la Pole, Joane, 4th Baroness Cobham 62, 66, 67, 68, 69, 70, 71, 202

229

Index

John 58, 59, 61, 62, 63, 67, 68, 202
Margaret 62, 63
Michael, 1st Earl of Suffolk 61
Richard 60, 61
William (3 generations) 59, 60, 61, 62, 63, 67, 69
de Longueville, John 67
Margaret 67
de Peyton, John 85, 103
de St. Armand, Alianore 67
Almaric 67
de Wacy, Ralph 2
de Yvele, Henry 53
Debenham 83
Delahoide, John 107
Delforce, Cedric 206
Denmark 1
Devenschir, Counte de 54
Devereux, Charles Robin de Bohun 201
Frances 94, 205
Penelope 93
Robert, 2d Earl of Essex 93, 94, 95, 112, 205
3d Earl of Essex 94
Robert Milo Leicester 201
Devon, Earls of: see Courtenay
Devonshire 45, 51
Dewey Ballantine 191, 192
Dewey, Thomas E. 191
Dexter, Missouri 170
Dietrich, Marlene 175
Donegal, Earl of 116
Donoghmoore Parish 120

Dorset 79
Dowell, Anne 135
Dowling, Patrick 216
Drayton 85
Drogheda 106, 113, 120, 121, 128, 210
Drogheda, Earls of xv, xvi, 106
Dublin Castle 148
Dublin Goldsmiths' Co. 99, 115, 117, 118, 125
Dublin, Ireland 99, 102, 106, 109, 110, 115, 116, 117, 118, 119, 121, 122, 125, 128, 131, 132, 133, 134, 135, 137, 140, 141, 145–150, 154, 157, 158, 163, 202, 211, 214, 215, 216, 217
Duchy of Normandy 13
Duke of Normandy 1, 2
Duluth, Minnesota 163–168, 171, 172, 173, 175, 176, 177, 178, 187, 218
Dungannon 111
Dunshaghlen, Co. Meath 107

Earls of Devon: see Courtenay
Earls of Essex: see Bohun and Devereux
Earls of Hereford: see Bohun
Eastmoreland Park, Dublin [Ireland] 150, 151, 152
Edenderry, Co. Kildare [Ireland] 121

Index

Edith, wife of Edward the Confessor 3
Edmund Ironside, King 2, 14, 17
Edward the Confessor, King 2, 3, 14, 17, 30
Edward I, King xiii, 22, 30, 32, 33, 34, 37, 38, 39, 41, 43, 60, 139, 201
Edward II, King 39, 41, 42, 43, 55, 60, 85, 103
Edward III, King 39, 42, 43, 46, 60, 61, 191
Edward IV, King 39, 83, 86
Edward V, King 39
Egbert, King 2
Eisenhower, Dwight David 192
Eleanor, of Acquitaine 11, 21, 23, 25, 31, 201
  of Provence 29, 30, 37, 201
  Princess, of Castile 37, 41, 201
Elizabeth Plantagenet, Princess xiii, 7, 41, 42, 43, 45, 201, 202
Elizabeth, Queen of Scotland 55
Elizabeth I, Queen 89, 90, 91, 92, 93, 94, 95, 101, 102, 105, 106, 107, 108, 112
Elizabeth II, Queen xiii, 94, 111, 194, 195, 205, 210
Elizabethtown Township, [Ontario] Canada 135, 151

Elliott, Anne 156, 157, 158, 160, 163, 165, 203
Ellis, Peter Berresford 212
Emma, Queen 2
Emmanuel College, Cambridge University 91
Emmett, Robert 148
Enniscorthy 126, 137
Equal protection 26
Erickson, Margaret Amelia 189, 191, 197
Ermengarde, of Anjou 6
Esmonde, — (Lt.) 122
  John 121
  Lord 121
Esquire, title 187
Essex 41, 58
Essex, Earls of: see Bohun and Devereux
Ethelred the Unready, King 2, 14, 17
Eustace, — 123
Evangeline's 195
Eveleth, Minnesota 175
Evelyn, Anne 80, 81, 83, 86
Evesham 30
Exeter 195
Exeter, England 46, 202

Fade, Dublin 215
Falaise 1
Falstaff, Sir John 70
Ferns, Co. Wexford [Ireland] 126, 129, 149
Fisher, — 128
  — (Capt.) 116
  — (Mr.) 187

Index

Edward, Sir 108, 109, 115, 116, 118, 120, 122, 210, 211
Elizabeth 116, 122
Henry 116, 210
John 210
Lettice 115, 117, 118, 119, 121, 122, 202
Mary 119, 120, 121
Fisher's Prospect 119, 122
Fitzgerald, Lord Edward 137
Fitzwalter, Earl 91
Flanders, Count of 4
Flintshire, Wales 41
Foman, Bob 193
Fontevraud 23, 31
France 1, 3, 5, 15, 21, 25, 45, 53, 70, 128
Francis, Deborah Ann 217, 218
  Hugh 85
  Margaret 84, 85, 86
French Revolution 5, 136
Fulk, Count of Anjou 14, 15
Furnivall 74

Galway, Connaught 95
Gardiner, Lord 190
Garter, Order of 93
Gascony 37
Gaveston, Piers 42
Gentry 134, 141, 145, 149
Geoffrey Plantagenet, Count of Anjou 6, 10, 15, 17, 18, 21, 23, 38, 39, 201
George III, King 135, 214
Gerhardt, W. F. 171
Germany 5, 169

Gifford's Hall, Wickham Brook 85
Giggins, — 211
  Katherine 116
Gillon, — 176
  Alfred 172, 173
  Angeline Hamilton 173
  Ann Kenny 163, 167, 172, 173
  Anna 173
  Carrie McNairnay 173
  Charlie 166
  Fanny 158, 160, 162, 163, 164, 165, 167, 172, 173, 203, 218
  Henry 163, 167, 172, 173
  Henry K. 172, 173
  James F. 172, 173
  Jane Speedie 173
  Letitia 173
  Lillian L. 173
  Robert J. 163, 167, 172, 173
Glorious Revolution 128, 129
Gloucestershire 73, 110
Godwine, Earl of Wessex 3
Gorey, Co. Wexford [Ireland] 119, 135, 137, 149
Great Britain 140, 171
Great Depression 175
Great Lakes 172
Great Lindford, Buckingham 105
Great Rebellion of 1641 120, 121, 126, 127
Grenville Co., Canada 158
Griffith, — (Mr.) 146
Gross, Leah 169

Index

Guedalla, Philip 215
Guild of Barber-Surgeons 134, 135, 141, 145, 146, 147, 153, 154
Gyrth 4

Habeus corpus 26
Hal, Prince 69, 70
Halstow 70
Hamilton, Angeline Gillon 173
Hampshire 26
Hanape, Joane 73
Haro: see Hero
Harold, King 3, 4
Harpenden, John 71
Harthacnut, King 3
Harvard 189, 191, 195
Hastings 4
Hawaii 171
Hawberk, John 69
  Nicholas 69
Hayne, Dorithie 190
Hemenhale, Robert 68
  William 68
Henry I, King 4, 5, 9, 10, 13, 14, 15, 17, 18, 21, 38, 201
  King of France 2
Henry II, King 11, 12, 20, 21, 22, 23, 25, 27, 31, 38, 39, 47, 51, 112, 201
Henry III, King 11, 12, 26, 27, 29, 30, 37, 39, 60, 67, 201
Henry IV, King 39, 43, 46, 54, 68, 69, 70, 102, 201

Henry V, German King and Holy Roman Emperor 17
  King 39, 71
Henry VI, King 80, 82, 208
Henry VII, King 39, 86
Henry VIII, King 91
Henry de Bohun, signer of Magna Carta 25, 42, 196
Henry of Bolingbroke 43, 201
Henry, Nelson B. 170
Herbert I, Count of Vermandois 6
Herbert II, Count of Vermandois 6
Hero
  Estelle Marguerite 171, 173, 174, 177, 178, 187, 203
  Joseph 176
  Michael 176
  Stanislaw Chara 175
  Stanley Chara 176
  Walter 173, 175, 176, 177
Hicklin, Wayne 193
Higham, Prioress of 63
Hockey 178
Holditch 73, 79, 80, 83, 208
Holland 93
Holy Roman Emperor 5, 15, 17
Hoo 70
Hopkins, Oceanus 190
  Stephen 190
Hore, Philip H. 211
Horton Farm, New Dublin, Ontario 142
Hotham 73

233

Index

Howard, Edward 135
Hugh Capet, King of France 7
Hull 59, 60, 61
Hull, Herbert 218
Humphrey de Bohun: see Bohun
Hutton, E. F. 193

Iceland 191
Ilchester 73, 208
Investment banking 60, 195
Ireland 92, 94, 95, 101, 103, 105, 107, 110, 111, 113, 125, 127, 128, 129, 135, 140, 151, 152, 153, 155, 159, 167, 171, 211
Isabella, of Angouleme 11, 25, 26, 29, 201
  of France 42, 47
Isle of Jersey 54, 68
Isleham, Suffolk 85, 86
Italy 5, 176

Jackson, Annis 218
  Charles J. 211
James I, King 43, 55, 103, 108, 111, 113, 115
James II, King 128
Jamestown, Virginia 190
Jefferson, Thomas 154
Jenyson, Thomas 101
Jerusalem 1
Joan 60
Joan, Lady of Cobham 66 and see de la Pole
  Countess of Gloucester 43

John, First Lord Beauchamp 51
  King 11, 23, 24, 25, 26, 27, 29, 39, 201
  Lord of Cobham 49 and see Cobham, 3d Baron
John I, Count of Holland & Zeeland 41
John of Gaunt 46
Johnson, Paul 212
Judith, of Brittany 7

Kennett, Missouri 166, 168, 170, 171, 172, 173, 175
Kenny, Ann: see Gillon James 163, 173
Kent 49, 50, 52, 65, 66, 70
Kevanaghe, Art McDermond 108
Kilcormack Parish 120
Kildahl, James 216
Killenagh Parish 120
King, Hannah 190
  Katherine 190
  Margaret Clarissa 180, 187, 189, 191, 195, 197, 203
  Mary 190
  Samuel 190
  Willard Leroy 189, 190, 191, 197
  William 188, 189, 190, 191
Kingston Bewsey, Sussex 106
Kinsale, Ireland 112, 113, 128, 136
Knight Banneret 45, 53, 79
Konczak
  Josephine 173, 176, 177

234

Index

Stanislaw (Stanley) 173, 176, 177
Kumble, Steve 189, 193

Laffer, Art 195
Lake Forest Academy 191
Lake Valley Cheese Factory and Farm 159
Lawrence, Sir Thomas 144
Lay, John [the Chaplain] 70
le Despenser, Hugh 42
Le Mans, Anjou, France 10, 18, 21
Lecky, — 133, 148
Leeds Co. Ontario 141, 158, 217, 218
Legal Times 194
Lehmberg, Stanford E. 209
Lennox, Dukes of 55
Lewknor, Alice 209
   Edward 106, 111, 209
   Eleanor 106
Lincoln 37
Lincolnshire 27, 43, 105
Lollards 70, 71
London 38, 60, 61, 92, 95, 103, 190
London, Bishop of 67
Lord, Eduard 171
Louis, Prince of France 27, 29
Louis Le Gros, King of France 47
Louis the Pious 5
Louis VII, King of France 23
Love, F. M. 172
Lower Blind Quay 117
Lublin, Poland 176

Lyon 15

Macbeth 15
Magna Carta 13, 25, 42, 196
Malcolm III, King of Scotland 14, 15
Manhattan 117
Manley, — (Gen. Count) 129
   Emelia Georgianna 129
Margaret, daughter of the Earl of Hereford 42
Margaret, Lady of Cobham 50 and see Courtenay
Marshall, William 29
Martyn, Clement 118
Mary-Ann 141, 153
Mary, Queen 128
Mary (Bloody), Queen 92
Matilda, Contess of Essex 42
Matilda, Empress 10, 14, 15, 17, 18, 21, 38, 39, 201
   of Flanders, wife of William the Conqueror xiii, 1, 4, 5, 7, 13, 201
   Princess of Scotland, wife of Henry I 13, 14, 201
Mayflower 190
Mayo Clinic 178
McBride, Jane 163, 173
McDonald, Bernard 217
Meaux 60
Mellifont 111, 113
Middelburg, Flanders 79
Might, — 102
Milan, Duke of 176
Mildmay, Benjamin 91
   Edward 91

235

Index

Joanne 91, 92, 101, 202
John 91
Margery 91
St. John 209
Thomas, Sir 87, 88, 91, 119
Walter, Sir 89, 91, 92, 101, 102, 113, 209
William 91
Molyneux, Thomas 106
Monamolin, Parish of 120, 153
Monasterevan, Co. Kildare [Ireland] 138
Moore, — 95, 128, 129
  Abner D. 158, 165
  Albert 158, 159
  Ann 159
  Anna 159
  Anne 135, 141, 143, 153, 154, 159, 210, 213
  Baron 214
  Charles Earls of Drogheda 111, 113, 120, 135, 140, 147
  Charles C. 173
  Charles Proctor 164, 168, 173
  Charles Ralph 168
  Charles Ralph Henry 185, 191, 197, 203
  Charlotte 157
  Claudia Lucille 168
  Daniel 135, 141, 149, 152, 153, 154, 213
  Derry 12th Earl of Drogheda xvi
  Edw. F. 133, 142, 148, 195, 212, 213, 214, 215, 217
  Edward 111, 218
  Edward Cooke Howard 132, 154
  Elizabeth Jane 135, 143
  Elizabeth Margaret Clarissa 184, 191, 197, 203
  Estelle: see Hero
  Fanny: see Gillon
  Fanny Ione 171
  Frances 159
  Frances Jane 158, 164, 167, 168, 217, 218
  Francis 159
  Francis Royal 157, 158, 159, 164
  Frederick 131, 135, 138, 141, 142, 143, 145, 149, 150, 151, 152, 154, 155, 214, 215, 216, 217, 218
  Garret Viscount and Earl 106, 110, 111, 113, 120, 210
  Harriet 159
  Harriet Anne 158
  Henry 111, 120
  Henry Francis 218
  Isabella 147, 158, 159, 160, 213, 214, 215
  John, Gen. Sir 149
  John 212, 218
  John B. 151
  John Francis 158, 168, 217, 218
  Keith Elliott 168
  Lorne Bruce 168, 218
  Lorraine Zulieka 168
  Louella Jane 168
  Margaret 135, 141, 143, 151, 154, 213
  Margaret Clarissa: see King
  Marilyn Estelle 177, 187

Index

Mark 147, 154–160, 163, 164, 165, 167, 203, 214, 215
Mark Alfred 160, 162, 163, 165, 167, 168, 173
Mark Hilton Ponsonby 168, 218
Mary A. 159
Mary Anne 158, 160, 165
Oliver 217
Proctor: see Walsingham Proctor
Ralph Henry 157, 163, 166, 167, 168, 170–176, 187, 203, 217, 218
Ralph Henry (Jack) 171, 173, 174, 175, 177, 178, 203
Richard 151
Rose Virginia 171
Sara 151
Sarah Anne 158
Sarah Elizabeth 186, 199, 203
Susannah 148
Thomas, Sir 110
Thomas Ronald 83, 105, 112, 177, 179, 181, 186, 187, 189, 191–197, 203
Walsingham 132, 135, 141, 142, 143, 145–155, 157, 158, 159, 178, 203, 212, 213, 214, 216, 217, 218
Walsingham Proctor 132, 150, 157, 158, 159, 160, 162, 163, 164, 165, 167, 203, 212, 216
Walter 209
Willard Sean 182, 191, 197, 203
William xiii, xvi, 131–136, 138, 141, 142, 143, 150, 151, 153, 155, 157, 158, 159, 203, 213–218
William F. 142
William Ponsonby 218
William Proctor 212
Williametta 168, 218
Moore Place, Kent 140
Morgan, Daniel 172
  George Cadogan 191
Morley, Derbyshire 126
Morris, Thomas 155, 159
Mortimer, Roger 42
Moulsham Hall 87, 91
Mountjoy, Lord (Charles Blount) 93, 95, 107, 112, 113
Mucrus, Co. Limerick, Ireland 102
Munster 112, 116
Murphy, John 137
Musgrave, — 138
  Richard 213

Napoleon xiii, 150, 152
National Society to Prevent Blindness (Prevent Blindness) 194
Navarre, King of 102
Nazi 176
Neiman, Ressie 170
Nelson, Margaret Else 183, 197, 203
New Dublin, Ontario, Canada 142, 160, 165
Newfoundland 152

Index

Newman, Alice 101, 103, 202
New York Hospital — Cornell Medical Center 191
Nicaea 1
Nobility 46, 136
Norfolk 68
Normandy 6, 14, 25
Northampton 61, 62, 83
Northamptonshire 67
Norway 1
Nottinghamshire 37

O'Connor, — 147, 148, 149, 203
O'Hart, John 129, 210, 212
O'Neill, Hugh 112
   Owen 120
Oldcastle, Joane 71
   John, Sir and Lord 69, 70, 71, 73
Ontario, Canada 135, 162, 172, 213
Order of St. Patrick 135
Oulart Hill 137
Oxford 23, 29

Paget 223
Pakenham, Kitty 149
Palmer, Anne 101, 103
Paris, Matthew 60
Parish, Joel 158
Parliament 38, 53, 55, 79, 81, 92, 128, 133, 139, 140
Parsons, — 123
   Arthur 125
   John 106, 119
   Walsingham 120, 121

William 106, 119
Peers 134
Peninsula Wars 149
Pepin, Count of Senlis, Peronne & St. Quentin 6
   King of Italy 6
Petrino, Michael 195
Peverel 71, 72
Peverel, John 67
   Margaret 61, 67
Peyton, — 128
   Anne xiii, xv, 83, 102, 103, 105, 106, 109, 110, 111, 112, 115, 117, 121, 202, 205, 210
   Christopher (2 generations) 85, 86, 90, 91, 92, 95, 97, 101, 102, 103, 105, 107, 109, 113, 202
   Cicilie 103
   Crystofer 86
   Elizabeth 103
   Frances 92
   Francis 83, 85, 86, 91, 202
   Henry 92
   John 85, 103, 104
   Martha 92
   Mary 92
   Thomas 85, 86, 92
   Thomasin 103
Phi Beta Kappa 191
Philip Augustus, King of France 27
Pigote, Robert 103
Piper, Poyntz 60
Plantagenet, Geoffrey: see Geoffrey

238

Index

Plantagenet, Princess Elizabeth xiii, 7, 41, 42, 43, 45, 201, 202
Plymouth 46
Plymouth Colony 190
Poitou 29
Poland 169, 173, 176, 177
Ponsonby, Sarah 218
Powderham Castle, Exeter 45, 46, 116, 202, 206
Power, Tyrone 175
Presov, Slovakia 169, 170
Pritchett, W. 208
Privy Council 94, 111
Proctor, — 129
   Frances (2 generations) 131, 132, 133, 134, 135, 145, 147–152, 155, 157, 158, 160, 163, 203, 213, 215
   Frances Cooke 154
   Frederick 131, 133, 203
   Jane 134
   Mary 134, 158
   Susannah 134, 147
   Thomas 128
   Walsingham 131, 132, 133, 134, 135, 145, 146, 147, 150, 151, 214, 215, 216, 217
Provence 29

Quebec, Canada 141, 142, 153
Quendon, Essex 41

Rathdrome 106
Rathecoole 102
Read, Agnes 91
Reading 15
Rebellion of 1798 134, 136, 137, 138, 139, 148, 149
Rebellion of Robert Emmett 148
Redburga 2
Redmond, — 129
   John Henry O'Byrne 129
   Magdelin 129
   Reginald Pius Rudolph Plantagenet 129
Rich, Lord 93
Richard II, Duke of Normandy 7
Richard II, King 39, 53, 54, 68
Richard III, King 39
Richard Lionheart, King 23, 25, 31, 39
Ring, George 193
Robert, Count of Meaux & Troyes 6
Robert Bruce, King of Scots 55
Robert Curthose Duke of Normandy 4, 13, 14
Robert I, King of France 6
Robert the Devil, Duke of Normandy 1, 7
Roche, Edward 148
   Walter 122
Rochelle 102
Rochester Castle 55
Rollo, Duke 1, 6
Rome 5
Roosevelt
   Franklin Delano 189, 192

Index

Rosenwater, Aaron 169
  Blanche Eloise 166, 167, 168, 170, 175, 203
  Ione 171
  Louis 168, 169, 170
  Samuel 169, 170
  Sarah 169
Ross
  James 156, 158, 160
  James (Mrs.) 147, 159, 160, 217
Rosse, Earl of 106, 119
Rotheram, Catherine 125
  Christopher 125
Rouen 5, 18
Rowse, A. L. 213
Rowsome, Samuel 135, 138
Royalty 134
Royston, Herts 207
Russell, William 106, 107, 112, 115
Russia 176
Ruvigny & Raineval, Marquis of 43
Ryalside, Massachusetts 190

Sacheverell, arms 100
Sacheverell, — 128
  Margaret 125, 126, 127, 203
  Mary 126
  William 126, 127, 128
Sadleir, — (Mr.) 215
Saint Louis, King of France 30, 194
Saint Margaret 14
Salem, Massachusetts 188, 189, 190

Salem, Oregon 173
Savoy 29
Schiller Park, Illinois 176
Scotland 45, 139
Scullabogue 137
Sedgrave, Patrick 107
Seymour, Jane 205
  William 205
Sforza, Bona 176
Shakespeare 15, 70, 190
Shenette, Lawrence 177
  Thomas Watts 177
  Toni Lynn 177
  Tracy 177
Sheviock, Cornwall 46
Shillelah, Ireland 158
Sicily 62
Sidney, Henry 110
  Philip, Sir 93, 94
Sikeston, Missouri 170
Sinclair, James 193
Sippican Corp. 193
Sleanagrane 129
Slievenegrane, alius Cookestowne 127
Smiths Falls, Ontario [Canada] 157, 164
Somerset 51, 79, 80
South Frederick St., Dublin [Ireland] 150
Southold, Long Island [New York] 190
Spanish Armada 93
Speedie, Jane Gillon 173
Spence School 191
St. Albans 82

Index

St. Amand, Third Baron 82
St. Barbe, Henry 106
  Margaret 92, 105
  Ursula 92, 105
St. Bartholomew's Day Massacre 93
St. James Episcopal Church 197
St. John of Jerusalem (The Most Venerable Order of The Hospital of) 194
Stamp Office 151
Steinhardt, Michael 195
Stephen, Count of Blois 4
  King 4, 18, 21, 38, 39
Story, George 150, 215, 216
Suffering Loyalists 134, 135, 138, 139, 141
Suffolk 41, 83, 103
Suffolk, First Duke of 61
Sutton, Hamon 85
  Joane 85
Symes, George 141

Taft 195
Taxation without representation, no 26
Taylor, George 213
TCI 193
Telluride, Colorado 195
Templars 55
Tese, Vincent 193
Thomas à Becket 20, 22
Thompson, J. Walter 193
Thorncombe 73, 79, 80
Tickell, Marston Eustace 123
Time-Life 191

Tomduff, Wexford 119, 120, 121, 125
Tomduff House 126
Tone, Wolfe 136, 139
Toronto, Canada 151
Touchet, Elizabeth 81
  James 81
  John 83
Touraine 25
Tours, battle of 5
Tower of London xviii, 38, 69, 71
Travis, J. E. 172
Treleboys, — (M.) 102
Trial by jury 26
Trinity College 145
Truman, Harry S 192
Tulane 195
Tyrconnel, Earl of 113
Tyrone, Earl of 95, 112, 113

Ufford Place, Suffolk 83
Ulster [Ireland] 112, 126, 136
Ulster King of Arms xiii, 126, 131, 223
Ulster, Plantation of 111, 113
United Church of England and Ireland 140
United Irish Society 136, 137, 149
United Kingdom 139, 140, 148, 152, 153
University of Chicago Laboratory School 191
Urban V, Pope 62
U. S. Army 171, 178, 187

241

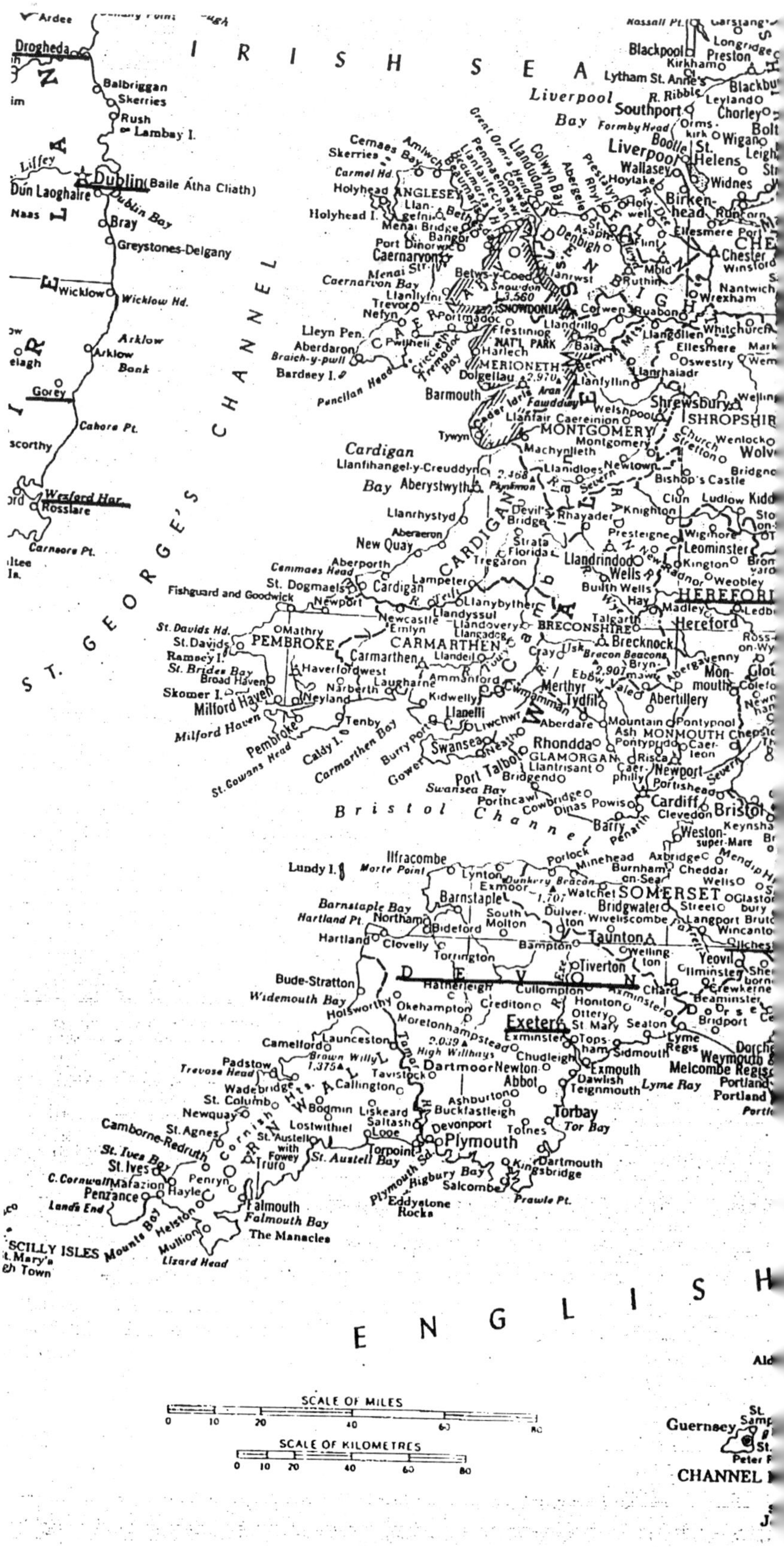